In tracing this rich, colour!
thread through the eventful
from 1066 to Margaret Thatcher, Robert Wardell, a
London Tourist Board Guide was inspired by one particular overseas visitor. On assuming that the statue of Queen
Anne in front of St Paul's Cathedral was that of Anne
Boleyn, she was gently corrected by the author: 'No, this
one died in 1794.' The young woman shrugged: 'One
Queen Anne is much the same as another.' This book was
written for her and for others like her who are frustrated
in their wish to appreciate the glorious British heritage
with its pageant of fascinating characters—simply because
they have forgotten what they once knew, or because, in
reading a general history book, sheer weight of detail
becomes ever more confusing.

With the elegance and humour of a master raconteur,
Robert Wardell guides us through the centuries, illumi-
nating with anecdote much that we take for granted. Set
firmly in the context of developments in religion, exploration, science and art, this clear and comprehensive
outline of English History spotlights the qualities of sturdy
independence, inventiveness and adaptability that are the
hallmark—and pride—of the Englishman.

Robert Wardell, author of 'Through a Coach Window', is
a Senior Tour Guide for London Transport, Holder of the
London Tourist Board Blue Badge and the Royal Society of
Arts Diploma in 'Road Transport'.

He worked in music publishing and at Harrods until
1970 when he joined London Transport as a tour guide.

His interests include music, bridge, cricket and 'being a
Yorkshireman'. He now lives in North London.

An Informal Guide to
English History

*From William the Conqueror to
Margaret Thatcher*

Robert Wardell

Temple House Books
Sussex England

For all my blue-badged colleagues throughout Britain whose enthusiasm, dedication and knowledge is so much appreciated by visitors to these shores.

Temple House Books
25 High Street,
Lewes, Sussex

First published 1987
© Robert B. Wardell 1987

Set in Linotron Cartier
Typeset by CST, Eastbourne
Printed in Great Britain by
Antony Rowe Ltd
Chippenham, Wilts

ISBN 0 86332 196 8

CONTENTS

thened. Start of Hundred Year War against France. Success of English archers at Battle of Crécy followed by rise of chivalry. Order of the Garter established in 1348. Death of the Black Prince. King Richard defeats Peasants' Revolt but is usurped by his cousin Henry, son of John of Gaunt. Henry V continues war against France and gains overwhelming success in 1415 at Agincourt.

ment not realised. General Strike of 1926. Troubles in Ireland and India. George the Fifth achieves popularity before his death. Edward the Eighth abdicates to marry an American, Mrs Simpson. Coalition governments rearm to meet threat from Hitler's Germany. World War II and Britain is saved by 'The Few'. Churchill emerges as a great wartime leader, the giant of his age. Darkness and defeat lead to final victory. Clement Attlee becomes Labour Prime Minister and develops both a comprehensive welfare state and governmental control of essential industries. Independence in India.

PRIME MINISTERS from 1727 to Present Day

Sir Robert Walpole	1727–1742	Whig
Lord Wilmington	1742–1743	Whig
Henry Pelham	1743–1754	Whig
Duke of Newcastle*	1754–1756	Whig
Duke of Devonshire	1756–1757	Whig
Duke of Newcastle	1757–1762	Whig
Lord Bute	1762–1763	Tory
George Grenville	1763–1765	Whig
Lord Rockingham	1765–1766	Whig
Duke of Grafton	1766–1770	Whig
Lord North	1770–1782	Tory
Lord Rockingham	1782	Whig
Lord Shelburne	1782–1783	Whig
Duke of Portland	1783	Whig
William Pitt (Pitt the Younger)	1783–1801	Whig
Henry Addington	1801–1804	Tory
William Pitt (Pitt the Younger)	1804–1806	Tory
Lord Grenville	1806–1807	Tory
Duke of Portland	1807–1809	Whig
Spencer Perceval	1809–1812	Tory
Lord Liverpool	1812–1827	Tory
George Canning	1827	Tory
Lord Goderich	1827–1828	Whig
Duke of Wellington	1828–1830	Tory
Earl Grey	1830–1834	Liberal
Lord Melbourne	1834	Whig
Sir Robert Peel	1834–1835	Conservative
Lord Melbourne	1835–1841	Whig
Sir Robert Peel	1841–1846	Conservative
Lord John Russell	1846–1852	Liberal
Lord Derby	1852	Conservative

Lord Aberdeen	1852–1855	Liberal
Lord Palmerston	1855–1858	Liberal
Lord Derby	1858–1859	Conservative
Lord Palmerston	1859–1865	Liberal
Lord John Russell	1865–1866	Liberal
Lord Derby	1866–1868	Conservative
Benjamin Disraeli	1868	Conservative
William Ewart Gladstone	1868–1874	Liberal
Benjamin Disraeli	1874–1880	Conservative
William Ewart Gladstone	1880–1885	Liberal
Lord Salisbury	1885–1886	Conservative
William Ewart Gladstone	1886	Liberal
Lord Salisbury	1886–1892	Conservative
William Ewart Gladstone	1892–1894	Liberal
Lord Rosebery	1894–1895	Liberal
Lord Salisbury	1895–1902	Conservative
Arthur Balfour	1902–1905	Conservative
Sir Henry Campbell-Bannerman	1905–1908	Liberal
Henry Asquith	1908–1915	Liberal
Henry Asquith	1915–1916	Coalition
David Lloyd George	1916–1922	Coalition
Andrew Bonar Law	1922–1923	Conservative
Stanley Baldwin	1923–1924	Conservative
Ramsay Macdonald	1924	Labour
Stanley Baldwin	1924–1929	Conservative
Ramsay Macdonald	1929–1931	Labour
Ramsay Macdonald†	1931–1935	Coalition
Stanley Baldwin	1935–1937	Coalition
Neville Chamberlain	1937–1940	Coalition
Winston Churchill	1940–1945	Coalition
Clement Attlee	1945–1951	Labour
Winston Churchill	1951–1955	Conservative
Harold Macmillan	1955–1957	Conservative
Sir Alec Douglas-Home	1963–1964	Conservative
Harold Wilson	1964–1970	Labour
Edward Heath	1970–1974	Conservative
Harold Wilson	1974–1976	Labour
James Callaghan	1976–1979	Labour

Margaret Thatcher   1979–   Conservative

Notes:
Political Party labels from 1727 to the mid-nineteenth century can be misleading if taken in the context of modern party systems; Prime Ministers and their supporters were more independent and their groupings could change and reform according to issues of the day.

*Between 1755–1762 William Pitt (known to us as Pitt the Elder or Earl of Chatham) was the most powerful member of the government although he was not the nominal Prime Minister.

†The coalition government between 1931 and 1940 was a 'government of national unity' although the composition was mostly Conservative. From 1940 to 1945 more Labour and Liberal politicians joined forces with the Conservative majority.

INTRODUCTION

Very recently an overseas visitor pointed to the statue of Queen Anne standing in front of St Paul's cathedral in London and asked who it was. 'Queen Anne' I replied. After a moment's hesitation she said 'Oh yes, Anne Boleyn, executed by Henry the Eighth'. Again I replied, gently I trust, 'No, this Queen Anne was the last of the Stuarts; she died in 1714'. The woman shrugged her shoulders: 'One Queen Anne is much the same as another.'

That young lady was my despair and my inspiration. For her this book was written.

It is not intended for the serious history student, someone who already knows a great deal and is hoping to discover a new interpretation of their own favourite period. Instead I want to reach those who wish to trace an uncomplicated thread through that exciting and eventful story we know as English History.

As a London Tour Guide I meet hundreds of overseas visitors every year. Many of them are frustrated in their wish to understand and appreciate what they experience, simply because they have forgotten what they once knew or because in reading a general history book the sheer weight of detail becomes ever more confusing.

Some of the attraction we feel towards English History is in the colourful personalities who are familiar to us since childhood. King Harold, who was supposedly shot in the eye at the Battle of Hastings; Richard the Lionheart; King Richard the Third, who may or may not have murdered the Princes in the Tower; Henry the Eighth and his six wives; Queen Elizabeth the First, often referred to as Good Queen Bess; Mary Queen of Scots; that merriest of monarchs, King Charles the Second; George the Third and his son the Prince Regent; Queen Victoria who gave her name to a whole way of life as she presided over the world's greatest empire; and our present Queen, surrounded by pageantry and a nation's love in equal measure.

Or perhaps your individual hall of fame contains Thomas a Becket, that 'turbulent priest' who became one of history's most enduring martyrs; Thomas Wolsey the butcher's son who rose to be Henry the Eighth's chancellor only to 'fall like lucifer' with even greater speed; Guy Fawkes; Oliver Cromwell; Nell Gwynne who sold King Charles not only oranges but her favours too; Sir Christopher Wren; Isaac Newton; Admiral Nelson who lost an arm and an eye but gained the love of his beloved Emma; the Duke of Wellington; William Wilberforce; Florence Nightingale and her memorable lamp; Lloyd George; and Churchill who needs neither a title nor first name to be identified as Britain's man of the century.

All these varied men and women populate the great set pieces of our history and invite either admiration or loathing but never indifference. It is they and the sturdy independance of this Island Race which provide the rich tapestry known to us as English History. And yet what do we mean when we say *English* History and when did it all begin.

So many of us say 'England' when we really mean something else, therefore it might be useful to make some definitions:

The United Kingdom is a political description of England, Wales, Scotland and Northern Ireland; in other words that area governed directly from our Parliament at Westminster.

Great Britain is a geographical description for that main island containing England, Wales and Scotland but excluding Ireland and the Isle of Man.

The British Isles is another geographical description; this time it embraces Great Britain, the whole of Ireland and all the off-shore islands.

England is, therefore, only a part, admittedly the largest and most important part, of a much bigger political and geographical area. *English* History does not cover the separate development and identities of Wales, Scotland or Ireland.

As to the beginning, this is a problem faced by all historians and no solution can ever be entirely satisfactory. Our history is such a long continuous story that, given time and unlimited patience of the writer and reader alike, the ideal moment would be when the land physically broke away from continental Europe. Slowly we would reach the point, five thousand years ago, when the first men arrived from that part of Europe now called Spain and Portugal. These, and later immigrants from Scandinavia, France and Flanders, were named 'Pretani' by those who came to trade in wine and tin; a word mispronounced by the Romans as 'Britani' or 'Britain'.

The Roman Occupation, beginning soon after the birth of Christ is another starting point, so would be the arrival of the Anglo-Saxons who filled a vacuum when the Romans left. In AD 686 the whole of England became Christian and Chapter One of any history book could usefully begin here. Later still, England was attacked and pillaged by Vikings and Danes and we enter the period of King Arthur and his knights of the round table, leaving their legendary stamp upon history or mythology. King Alfred the Great, founder of the Royal Navy, he of the burnt cakes, turned the tide against the Danes in 878, although it was Alfred's grandson, Athelstan, who might claim to be the first king of all England. That claim is disputed by supporters of Edgar, he had the honour of being *crowned* King of England inside Bath Abbey on 11th May 973. Interestingly enough the coronation service used then forms the basis of coronations ever since, including that of our own Queen in 1953. That fact alone might justify any historian to begin his Chapter One in Bath Abbey.

Further invasions by the Danes led to several of their number themselves being accepted as Kings of England; one of the most famous being Cnut (or Canute), who was persuaded to try and reverse the tides around these shores. King Canute died in 1035. After a brief power struggle that was both bloody and wearisome, Edward the Confessor became the king in 1042.

It is the events following his death which so decisively changed the course of English History. This is where I have chosen to begin.

1

THE NORMANS (1066 to 1154)

Ask any English schoolboy to mention just one date in English History and he will reply 'Ten Sixty-Six'. Why is that date so important to him? Is it because from that date our kings began to be numbered as well as named, making identification so much easier, or is there more to 1066 than that?

The year began unpromisingly with the death of Edward the Confessor. He had been the undisputed King of England for over twenty years, reigning over a country that was at peace with itself and with its neighbours. Even the Vikings and Danes stopped their raiding parties from pillaging and plundering on the scale they had earlier. The Anglo-Saxon tragedy was that Edward the Confessor did not take advantage of the peace to impose his authority and establish laws and tax-gathering that would benefit everyone. He might have been the king by royal descent but he did not rule as one.

As a young man he had lived as a monk in Normandy, his only enthusiasm being for religion hence his name 'Confessor' meaning a pious or holy man. Although destined to be revered as a saint by many future kings, his place in history now is that of a man who neglected kingly duties in favour of religion, allowing rival noblemen to quarrel between themselves and impose on their underlings whatever brand of justice they thought fit. Whether we call the eleventh century Anglo-Saxons relaxed and easy going, or merely undisciplined, is a matter of taste. The net result was just the same. England was too disorganised to withstand a crisis that could and should have been anticipated.

On 5th January 1066 King Edward the Confessor died peacefully in the new Palace of Westminster. As befitting a holy man his marriage had been celibate and he left no sons to succeed him. He did, however, leave two lasting memorials to his name. One is Westminster Abbey and the second is the site for our Houses of Parliament.

When Edward became king in 1042, he set himself the task of building a great abbey church. Because it was erected two miles west of the City of London, it became known as the West Monastery or West Minster Abbey. King Edward's tomb is the focal point, the shrine, of the present abbey church. To remain close during the building of this great abbey he decided to live within its shadow, bring his court officials and advisers (known as the Witan or 'wise men') to that wet marshy ground we now call Westminster. Thus, he removed his direct influence from the City of London, allowing the merchants and bankers to develop an independance of their own two miles from the seat of administrative and legislative power. Parliament in the form we now know would come later, but, as a one-time royal home of kings, the Parliament buildings are still, officially, The Palace of Westminster, and they are still within the very shadow of Westminster Abbey.

From his deathbed Edward the Confessor proclaimed Harold, son of a powerful but non-royal earl called Godwin, to succeed him. The Witan agreed and confirmed Harold as King of England. Both Edward and the Witan chose to ignore Edgar Atheling, even though he was the nearest male relative and by all hereditary principles had the prior claim. Edgar was brushed aside because he was a young boy and had no powerful friends to support him. As a result, two other contenders staked their claim. Both might have accepted Edgar as king; neither would accept Harold—and each declared their own claim was stronger.

William, Duke of Normandy was not only militarily powerful, he was also familiar with the intricacies of foreign politics. His claim was tenuous, to say the least, although two years earlier in 1064, when Harold was held prisoner in Normandy, William had secured a promise to be recognised as king when Edward died. Promises extracted under duress are frequently broken and such was the case when Harold found himself crowned king.

King Harald Haardraade of Norway also felt he had a claim

greater than anyone other than young Edgar Atheling, and he became the first to test the resolution of King Harold and his Anglo-Saxons. Moreover he had gained a useful ally in Harold's own brother, Tostig, who now supported Harald Haardraade and the Viking cause.

The Vikings (or Norwegians if you prefer the nearest modern equivalent) began by plundering the coast of eastern England; Tostig playing a leading part. Eventually, in September 1066, the Vikings invaded in strength and captured York. King Harold probably feared an invasion by William of Normandy more than he did the Vikings but the loss of York proved unacceptable and he led his army 200 miles north. With comparative ease he defeated the combined force of Harald and Tostig, killing them both. The battle took place at a river crossing six miles east of York; Stamford Bridge.

William of Normandy chose the same moment to turn his threatened invasion into reality. He crossed the channel and landed on the English coast at Pevensey on 28th September, consolidating and strengthening his bridgehead. Harold hurried south again and at once revealed his lack of skill as a military strategist. Numerically, his forces were superior to William's, but his army was less well equipped and he possessed neither cavalry nor archers to match the Normans. He could have waited to allow his army time to recover from a rapid march north and an even quicker return south. He could have waited to assemble more fighting men from the countryside, creating a force big enough to overwhelm the accurate bowmen and mobile horsemen by sheer numbers. In the event he did neither, preferring to seek an immediate confrontation.

On Saturday 14th October 1066, the two armies met on a hill near a village now called Battle. Seven miles distant lay Hastings, and it is this town which gave its name to the fighting: The Battle of Hastings.

Accounts of battles fought long ago can be tedious, especially when the details are probably inaccurate, always bearing in mind that the victors usually leave to posterity their own version of events. The Battle of Hastings differs in one important respect. Soon afterwards a tapestry was woven at Bayeux in Normandy, at the instigation of William's half-brother. It is now prized as a great work of art and has been accepted as a fair record of what actually happened, what the participants wore, and what weapons were used. It depicts not only the ebb and flow of battle as men belaboured each other with swords, axes, clubs and all manner of instruments both sharp and blunt, it also tells us of the circumstances surrounding the death of Edward the Confessor.

Contemporary accounts and the tapestry all agree that the issue was never in doubt. William was a superb fighter and what he lacked in numbers he made up in equipment, mobility and, above all, leadership. Even so, the battle was hard fought, with William himself in mortal danger on more than one occasion. Only in one respect does the Bayeux Tapestry leave a truly misleading impression: it created the legend of Harold killed by an arrow shot into his eye. This is due to an early misinterpretation of tapestry and most historians now agree he was killed by the sword. Nevertheless, once a legend gains credence truth takes second place.

Only now did the Witan proclaim young Edgar Atheling as king. It was seen as no more than a futile gesture. William was marching towards London and in no mood to recognise a boy as ruler of the kingdom he himself was about to conquer. Many brave Anglo-Saxons resisted the Normans in a disorganised fashion, but this only delayed the advance without stopping it.

Eventually, after much bloodshed, on Christmas Day 1066 William of Normandy, William the Conqueror, was crowned King William the First of England. His coronation took place in Westminster Abbey as he knelt reverently beside the tomb of Edward the Confessor. Tradition was thus established for all future sovereigns to be crowned in Westminster Abbey, close to the bones of King Edward.

For the next five years William's army of Normans, numbering around 12,000, employed every ruthless skill to subdue any native Anglo-Saxon who offered resistance—Hereward the Wake, in eastern England, being among the last to accept defeat. Conqueror though William undoubtedly was, he ruled as the rightful king of an established country which had clearly defined boundaries to be defended, and spurned any notion of turning his new possession into a satellite of Normandy. What sort of country was it he inherited, what changes did he make, and what were the consequences for future generations?

The population of England in 1066 totalled one and a half million, and under Edward the Confessor it was a Christian country with simple churches in every village, many of which survive to the present day. This Christianity had an organisation and hierarchy of its own, providing centres of learning, culture and healing of the sick. Some of the bishops and prelates were members of the Witan and shared with noblemen the responsibility for advising the king and ruling the country. There were cities of power and importance; ports that traded in wine, spices and silk; and agriculture to feed the populance, farmed by a stock of healthy Anglo-Saxon men and women, who worked the land for their aristocratic masters. The entire country was divided into shires—as it still is today—and the law-enforcement official in each shire was called a reeve; a combination of words from which we derive the word shire-reeve or sheriff.

Some of William's changes were physical and immediate. Townsfolk viewed with alarm the vast earthworks being thrown up on which Normans built castles of wood or stone. Castles that would serve as protection for his army as they marched and counter-marched across the kingdom quickly became prisons for any dissidents who dared to defy the new regime. Cathedrals and churches to dwarf the homely Anglo-Saxon places of worship also appeared. Durham Cathedral, Tower of London and a whole host of castles remain today as proof of the lasting quality of Norman building skill.

Other changes were more dramatic although less visible. The easy-going relationship between many workers and their lords was swept away when William deprived them later of their estates, as a punishment for daring to resist his seizure of a kingdom he judged his by right. William was now free to create an aristocracy from his Norman army, granting them land taken from the Anglo-Saxon nobility. These new barons imposed a different, continental method of enforcing land workers to toil for them, a complicated practice we now call 'the feudal system'. In simple terms this became a gradation of serfs, villeins and tenants who laboured for their Norman lord, paid him homage, and in return were protected by him and subjected to his own brand of justice. The barons in their turn pledged allegiance to King William and agreed to provide men and resources to protect and maintain the kingdom. At its lowest level the feudal system was harsh, restrictive, and even cruel, stopping only just short of outright slavery.

A lasting proof of King William's organisational genius was, and still is, the Domesday Book; 'domesday' meaning day of justice rather than retribution or impending tragedy. The book became a detailed census of the conquered people and an inventory of every part of his kingdom; every town, village, parish and plot was evaluated and itemised to give substance to William's conquest. Even present-day place names familiar to us find an entry in the Domesday Book, and by some miracle, it still survives and can be seen at the Public Record Office in London.

Another factor that has had unforeseen consequences concerned the English Language. Normans continued, of course, to speak French and the clergy used both Latin and French as their working language. The educated gentry considered it vulgar to speak Anglo-Saxon and for almost three hundred years it remained an unwritten language, spoken only by the common people who comprised over ninety per cent of the population. Thus the language grew and lived, without the doubtful 'help' of pedants and academic rules of grammar. It avoided the clumsy continental use of gender, and instead was free to express a nation's ideas in words and phrases that were direct, colourful and rich in meaning. Inevitably it absorbed some of the French vocabulary, some Latin, and the resultant outcome was that, in time, it re-entered polite society and flowered as the working tool of Chaucer, Shakespeare, Milton and Keats.

When William the First died in 1087, near Rouen in Normandy, he had created in England a country that was highly disciplined and organised. Not only was he the undisputed king, but he ruled with the confidence of knowing he owned England, every square inch of it, and that he owed no-one any favours or debts of gratitude. The Viking raids were almost a thing of the past. The borders of Wales and Scotland still had to be stoutly defended against raids in strength but the transformation was all too evident. Scandinavia was now a spent force, unable to threaten mainland Europe, simply because England, no longer a stepping stone or spring-board but a secure barrier against the Viking's continental ambitions was, at last, free to develop as an independant nation.

At the time of King William's death he had three sons; Robert the eldest, William, and Henry. Robert had taken little part in the conquest of England and his father regarded him as disloyal and rebellious. As a result, he was bequeathed the lesser prize of staying on the continent as Duke of Normandy. William, second son of the Conqueror, had always been a royal favourite and so he was crowned King William the Second. Because of his ruddy cheeks and flaming red hair he was known as William Rufus.

England's new king began his reign with a crisis. His elder brother Robert, feeling himself disinherited, threatened to invade with a second Norman Conquest and take England from William Rufus. The country might well have become disunited because Robert, as William the Conqueror's eldest son, had a strong claim and many supporters. However, the Archbishop of Canterbury, called Lanfranc, rallied to William Rufus and his example persuaded the population to accept and support William the Second as their lawful and undisputed king. Lanfranc proved to be a good influence on William Rufus and it was only when Lanfranc died two years later, in 1089, that the king seemed to reveal his true character.

Almost overnight King William gained the reputation he has kept ever since: an evil, foul-mouthed, arrogant king.

Few of the chronicles from those days are very specific as to why he deserves such infamy. He was certainly a homosexual and his overtly effeminate friends were no credit to him. He enclosed more and more land for his private recreation and hunting, thus depriving many country-dwellers of their homes and traditional sources of animal meat. However it was probably his contempt for the church and his public abuse of its clergy and officials that caused the greatest resentment. He appointed unsuitable bishops, or no bishops at all, confiscating their revenues and church taxes for his own purposes. His undisguised scorn for the established church and its dignitaries almost threatened the roots of Christianity itself. At times his enforcement of law and order had the appearance of being fair and firm, until his own interests were involved. He rarely punished his friends or soldiers when they were accused of mistreating the peasantry, although he tortured and frequently castrated those who offended him, regardless of their rank or title.

Only when fighting and leading his army did he win general approval. He drove the Scots from northern England, taking the city of Carlisle and the province of Cumberland as an extension of England's border. In Wales he was less successful, and his occasional raids into Normandy were equally inconclusive in spite of his personal bravery.

William Rufus is now remembered for two physical landmarks that have endured. Westminster Hall, the 240 foot long stone building almost underneath Big Ben, is his creation. So is the New Forest, a pleasantly wooded area about 80 miles south west of London.

It was in that New Forest, on 2nd August 1100, at a spot now marked by the Rufus Stone that King William the Second was accidentally killed whilst hunting. His body was humped, dripping with blood, to Winchester Cathedral a few miles distant. Here he was buried with the minimum of pomp and ceremony, although his simple tomb is impressive enough to modern eyes.

Henry, the younger brother of Rufus, showed his character and initiative at once. He was close to the scene of the accident and immediately siezed the royal treasure chest and in great haste had himself proclaimed King of England and crowned. Haste was vital if only because the older brother Robert, Duke of Normandy, still felt aggrieved at not being given the crown of England when his father William the Conqueror had died, and now he saw yet another junior brother crowned as King Henry the First of England.

Although not lacking courage King Henry preferred using his diplomatic skills before resorting to force. He fought only when intrigue, cunning and coercion had failed. Because he was able to read and write, a rare attribute at that time, even among kings, he became known as *Henry Beauclerc* (Henry the Clerk). Born in England, after his father's conquest, he could claim to be a native

Englishman, and he further cemented himself to his country when he married Princess Matilda, whose father was a Scottish king and whose mother was an English princess.

Furthermore, he imprisoned William Rufus's chief minister, Ranulf Flambard, and confined him in the Tower of London as an indication of disapproval at the way Rufus had misruled his kingdom.

King Henry the First distinguished himself by enforcing laws that attempted to be fair and even-handed. Not only that but he gained the confidence and respect of the church, restoring Christianity to an esteem it had lost during the reign of his brother. He also encouraged merchants and traders to adopt the codes and standards then developing on the continent and a lasting consequence was a mutual trust in which promissory notes were recognised by a third party; an early form of what we now call a cheque.

At this period of England's history, and for many centuries afterwards, wars, both internal and overseas, were not total in the modern sense. Merchants saw no need to cease trading because kings and princes were disputing each other's territory. They soon developed an independence which kings had to take into account.

Meanwhile Robert, Duke of Normandy, remained a threat. Undoubtedly he possessed a certain charm and a casual approach to life even though his closest friends were less charming and less casual. Together they succeeded in encouraging a minor revolt in England against King Henry and the inevitable result was a pitched battle in Normandy between the two brothers. For the first time ever, English archers showed how good they were and their skill secured a victory for Henry. Robert was captured and remained a captive for the remaining twenty-eight years of his life, dying in prison at the age of eighty.

King Henry was at the height of his power when disaster struck. In 1120 he was returning from Normandy to England and he allowed his son, William, to travel independantly on the finest ship then in the royal navy the White Ship. Just beyond the harbour at Barfleur the ship hit a rock and sank, drowning William and almost everyone else on board. King Henry almost died of grief when told of his son's death. It was said he never smiled again. Certainly his jester Raheere found himself unemployed and after a religious vision Raheere built a monastery in London dedicated to Saint Bartholomew. Not only does the church survive today but the hospital attached also remains, famous the world over by its abbreviated nickname 'Barts'.

The king's wife had already died and although he married again his new wife produced no children. Therefore his daughter Matilda was nominated as heir to the throne, a decision which Henry's noblemen supported.

In 1135 King Henry the First died in France at the age of sixty-seven. All but the first six years of his long reign had been peaceful and prosperous. Admittedly, he gained the reputation of being a womaniser and his personal morals were not of the highest; nevertheless compared with the nineteen years misery that followed, King Henry's reign had been golden.

The trouble stemmed from the character of Henry's daughter and heir Matilda. At the early age of nine she had been married to the Holy Roman Emperor—the Empire being a ramshackle disjointed chunk of Europe that would eventually disintegrate into a pattern of several diverse countries. When the Emperor died, Matilda married a French nobleman, Geoffrey Plantagenet Count of Anjou, and they produced a son, Henry.

Matilda, always fearless, became more dominant and demanding. The prospect of submitting themselves and the kingdom to such a woman dismayed many nobles who had earlier endorsed Matilda as King Henry the First's successor. They now decided to ignore her and offer the crown of England to Matilda's cousin, Stephen, the son of Henry's sister Adela, who had married Stephen of Blois. King Stephen never had a chance of success, lacking ambition, diplomatic skill, and the driving urge to rule like a king. His sense of duty was enough to make him brave in battle but insufficient to create either popular support or combat the ferocity of Matilda.

From 1135 onwards England was plunged into a civil war that became ever more bloody and confused. For nineteen bitter years anarchy prevailed unchecked. As Matilda gathered support in Normandy and then invaded from the south, her Scottish sup-

porters massed in the north, surging over the border to uphold
the honour of Matilda, remembering she was the grandaughter of
a Scottish king through her mother. Not wishing to miss an
opportunity the Welsh also attacked, from the west. In the
ensuing civil war everyone lost, especially the innocent peasantry
and townsfolk who desired only to be left in peace. It was a time,
according to a much-quoted chronicler, when 'God and his saints
slept'. In all its long history England had never endured such a
lengthy period of unmitigated horror and it would never sink
quite to such depths again.

The deadlock was broken when King Stephen's eldest son died,
and it was agreed that whilst Stephen would continue as king, his
younger son would not succeed him and that Matilda's son Henry,
by her second marriage, would eventually become king. A year
later, in 1154, King Stephen died and the way was clear for
Matilda's son to ascend the throne as King Henry the Second.

Stephen was the last Norman king of England. As Henry,
though Norman by descent, had already adopted his father's
name he now became the first of a long line of Plantagenet kings
of England. The name comes from a yellow flower worn in his
helmet, a flower sharing the same name as his father's French
family; *Plantagenet*.

A new era in England's history had begun. William the
Conqueror had demonstrated what could be achieved by strong,
sometimes ruthless, leadership. King Henry the Second, grandson
of Henry the First and therefore a great grandson of William the
Conqueror was now poised to restore law and order into a
country weary of strife, bitterness and black anarchy.

2

BECKET TO MAGNA CARTA (1154 to 1216)

To understand and appreciate what happened next it is important to see the institutions of the Church, marriage and family
relationships as the people of the time would have seen them. By
making judgements based on modern morality and ideas so much
of what happened in early English history is open to misinterpretation.

First the Church: Long before 1066 the Church had become an
indispensable factor in governing England. Bishops and prelates
shared with noblemen the responsibility for advising the king,
whilst the junior clergymen administered the country rather as
civil servants do today. This was because the clergy comprised the
educated class, able to read and write in an age when even kings
might be illiterate. In return for these services the clergy were
granted immunity from the king's law, and laws enforced locally
by land-owning earls. Instead the clergy instituted their own
ecclesiastical courts where punishments seldom fitted the crime.
Even deacons—unordained church officials—were free from the
king's jurisdiction and the privilege became widely abused. So
much so that *anyone* who could read or write claimed trial by the
weak ecclesiastical court: the criterion for such a privilege was no
more than an ability to read the first verse of the 51st psalm.

Not only was each king dependent on the Church to admin-
ister his kingdom and collect his taxes, but he was in even greater
need of the Church to grant him divine and spiritual guidance.
The Church, of course, was 'the Church universal' whose bishops
owed their allegiance directly to the Pope in Rome. For a king to
interfere with the power of the Church was to risk excom-
munication—in effect denying himself and his soul access to

God—and such a risk was terrifying for any mortal whether a king or not. It would be no exaggeration to say that every king was, to some extent, accountable to the Pope and needed courage to take any action which might be disapproved of in Rome.

Marriage was not straightforward either. It could, on occasion, be entered into for love but more usually kings married to gain some advantage for themselves or their kingdom. Political alliances and the acquisition of land were frequently the reasons for royal marriages. A king thus married to a woman he did not love would feel free to take a number of mistresses who might, possibly, produce several bastards. Even if this womanising was not generally approved of it was accepted as normal, if only as a sign of virility and manhood. In any case some marriages were contracted when the two participants were mere infants and neither party were expected to take such unions seriously when they became adults.

In an age when marriages could be as unromantic as a bill of sale, it is not surprising that family loyalties counted for nothing. In royal households father fought son and brother fought against brother with the kind of bloody ferocity we now reserve for our worst enemies. Intrigue, betrayal and unlawful killings—even of women and children if they stood in the way of inheritance or title—became almost an extension of kingship with some monarchs. Among rulers struggling to seize or maintain power, such wickedness could be perpetrated with neither conscience nor remorse. By contrast, only the peasantry, townsfolk and less powerful noblemen could afford the luxury of honesty and genteel morality.

All these elements of religious privilege, an unwise marriage, family disloyalty and brutal murder played their part in the life of our next king.

During the autumn of 1154, King Henry the Second was crowned in Westminster Abbey. He was twenty-one years old and possessed of a restless energy and physical endurance that exhausted his companions. For his time he was considered something of an intellectual, surrounding himself with poets of a serious nature, philosophers, theologians and travellers with experience of far-distant countries.

He began with a colossal stroke of good fortune. Matilda, his mother, decided to curb her own forceful nature and leave the stage entirely to her son. Henry was thus free to stamp his own character on the kingdom without Matilda's influence. His first task was to restore order from the anarchy which had stemmed from King Stephen's weakness and Matilda' belligerence. In only three years King Henry devised a system of government that would function efficiently, independent of the king's personal presence. Business confidence returned and records show that during Henry's thirty-five year reign the national income doubled.

Had he not been a king, Henry could have become an outstanding lawyer and he used his legal knowledge to reform England's laws and to create the machinery for them to be effective throughout his kingdom. It was Henry who sent judges to travel the country in a circuit, bringing a uniform justice to every quarter instead of the population having to rely on the whims, foibles and upredictable judgements of their local lords. Because King Henry's justice became common from one end of England to the other, it formed the basis of what we still call 'Common Law'. He also devised an appeals procedure in which irregularities during trials could be rectified, and with some modification this system is identical with the one we use today. The king himself frequently settled disputes in person between his subjects, and in particular he was recognised as an authority in cases of forgery. So great was his judicial reputation that he acted as referee between continental rulers and his judgements were accepted without question.

Nevertheless, King Henry had a weakness, an Achilles' heel: he was, quite simply, a poor judge of character. This led him into an unfortunate marriage and his celebrated conflict with Thomas a Becket.

Becket was born in London although his family originated in Normandy. He was well-educated, and he travelled widely in France and Italy before being ordained into the church and becoming secretary to the Archbishop of Canterbury. King Henry noticed the young man and appointed him Chancellor, virtually his closest adviser. Their relationship was intimate, almost like brothers, and in matters both personal and public they were in accord; or so it seemed. When the Archbishopric of Canterbury fell vacant King Henry appointed Becket, intending, no doubt, to reform the unfair ecclesiastical courts and so end the system of allowing clergymen to be above the king's law. Becket, as the king's friend, would be the ideal figure to rectify this anomaly from within the Church, except that Becket, the king's friend, was not the same man as Becket, Archbishop of Canterbury.

Almost overnight, Thomas a Becket began to defend the Church and defy the king as the old friendship faded into memory. King Henry was understandably frustrated and whether he actually exclaimed 'Who will rid me of this turbulent priest?' is now open to debate. The effect of the king's open dissatisfaction with his new Archbishop was that on 29th December 1170, four knights loyal to King Henry went to Canterbury Cathedral and there murdered Becket in cold blood. Christendom was enraged and the Pope was so incensed that King Henry was obliged to endure public penance, being whipped and scourged to assuage his mortal sin. The Church had gained a martyr in Becket to give itself even greater power and independence.

When he was eighteen years old, Henry had married a woman of thirty, Eleanor of Aquitaine. She had previously married the king of France, been divorced, yet even at thirty was considered one of the most beautiful women in Europe. The marriage cannot be regarded as successful, even though initially it was a genuine love-match which produced four sons and three daughters. He was serious and studious; she was carefree and convivial. Their clash of personalities doomed the marriage to endless bickering and arguments. Henry resorted to imprisoning Eleanor for twelve years whilst he took as his mistress a famous beauty, Rosamond de Clifford; 'the fair Rosamond'.

Eleanor had brought to her marriage with Henry the vast territory of Aquitaine, virtually the whole western seaboard of France. King Henry therefore became the ruler of an empire stretching a thousand miles from England's border with Scotland through Normandy (which he had inherited from his mother) to Aquitaine's border with Spain at the Pyranee mountains. However, the imprisoned Eleanor sought to regain control over

Aquitaine and she incited her eldest son, Richard, to join the king
of France and fight King Henry for it. So, not for the first time,
nor indeed the last, an English prince decided to wage war on his
father, and began a conflict between England and France that
would continue, on and off, for many hundreds of years.

Although King Henry had already given Scotland a crushing
defeat in an earlier campaign, reducing that land to be little more
than a vassal-state of England, on the continent he was less
successful. His son Richard was a sound general and brave fighter,
earning for himself the title 'Richard the Lionheart' by which he is
still known. Almost to add insult to injury Henry's youngest son,
John, lent his support to Richard and together they forced their
father to accept crushing peace terms: within weeks King Henry
was dead and many would say he died of a broken heart.

Henry the Second's bitter defeat on the mainland of Europe,
and his humiliations following the martyrdom of Thomas a
Becket, sometimes overshadow his great achievement in transforming the laws and machinery of government. For the people
of England his reign had been peaceful, prosperous and kindled an
appetite for justice they would never lose.

When Henry died in 1189 his eldest son, Richard the Lionheart
was crowned as his successor.

Although born in Oxford, he spoke little English and cared
nothing for the country of his birth. Richard was king for almost
ten years but during his reign spent less than six months in
England. His great ambition was to take Jerusalem and the Holy
Land from the Saracens and he joined other European rulers in a
mighty crusade. From this endeavour he gained the romantic
reputation he never lost and his posthumous reward is to have his
statue in a place of honour outside the Houses of Parliament in
London.

For the people of England he did nothing but tax them to
sustain the indulgence of a foreign adventure. He also left behind
him a power vacuum which proved a good test of his father's
system of smooth government, designed to work even when the
king was abroad, and work it did. Most successfully. For one thing
the offices of Chancellor and Treasurer were now permanently
established in London, instead of perambulating inefficiently

around the country. For another, a number of able and accomplished administrators guided the country's affairs; Hubert Walter and William Marshall would have been outstanding in any age.

Richard's younger brother, John, saw his opportunity for self-advancement and treachery during the king's absence. Again in alliance with the king of France he attempted to seize continental territory for himself, being thwarted mainly by his mother Eleanor who was now free to protect the interests of her favourite son, Richard.

It was during this period, when England's king was away, that two legends took root. The first is of Robin Hood who protected many peasants from oppressive and opportunist lords during a time when common law was not fully established. There is no firm evidence that Robin Hood even existed and the truth is probably that a number of 'Robin Hoods' sprang up in widely separated parts of the country. The second unsupported legend concerns that of Blondel, King Richard's troubadour. Richard was returning home through Austria when he was taken prisoner and his whereabouts became unknown. Blondel then serenaded every castle in Europe until his royal master recognised the minstrel's voice, showed himself, and Blondel returned with ransom money to secure King Richard's release. Blondel's serenading and Robin Hood are just two of the legends that enrich English History and all historians find the lack of corroboration disappointing.

Richard the Lionheart eventually returned from the Crusades with his wife, Berengaria, whom he had married on the island of Cyprus. At once he sought battle against the king of France to regain his lost territory, but in April 1199 he was killed by an arrow when he carelessly went into action without his armour.

King Richard died as he had lived; gallant, generous but never happier than when fighting or in conflict. In the mainstream of English History he is an irrelevance who paved the way for his brother John.

John was elsewhere in Normandy when he heard of Richard's death but before he returned to London for his coronation there was a small problem to be resolved. By the strict rules of primogeniture— hereditary rights to title—he was not the direct heir. Midway in age between Richard and John was their brother

Geoffrey, recently killed jousting in a tournament; it was his son, Prince Arthur, Duke of Brittany, a boy of thirteen when Richard was killed, who held the prior claim. Even so, John found it easy to persuade Hubert Walter, the Archbishop of Canterbury, and other senior barons to accept his claim rather than the boy's. Arthur himself appeared to accept the situation and thus on 27th May 1199 King John was crowned in Westminster Abbey.

If Richard the Lionheart's reputation has been inflated by romantics down the ages, John's has probably suffered too far in reverse. Numbered among England's very worst kings many of his qualities have been overlooked. He was a first class administrator himself and he surrounded himself with some very proficient ministers: Hubert Walter; William Marshall; Geoffrey Fitz Peter and Hubert de Burgh were wise and able in an age when such men were scarce. He rode tirelessly throughout his kingdom and was quick to discipline sherrifs when he found them wanting. He respected the laws and institutions begun by his father, Henry the Second, and as a practising Christian he supported the Church and was known for his generosity to the poor. It was John who was known as King of *England* instead of King of the Anglo-*Normans* as his predecessors had been and from his reign it is both convenient and correct to speak of the *English* rather than *Anglo-Saxons*.

John married twice and enjoyed the company of several mistresses. His first wife was English, Isabella, and when John tired of the marriage he persuaded his bishops to annul it. His second bride was Isabelle, a girl of twelve (some accounts say she was only eleven), and she was the daughter of an influential nobleman from Aquitaine and together John and his child-bride produced two sons and three daughters.

From the beginning of his reign King John found himself at war on the continent, fighting to maintain Normandy, Aquitaine and Anjou against the increasingly ambitious French king. At first John was successful and when he heard news that his aged mother, Eleanor of Aquitaine, was besieged in her castle at Mirebeau he came to her rescue. The besieging army was led by a mere youth, who proved to be Prince Arthur, now sixteen years old and still the rival claimant to the English throne. There is a strong suggestion that King John himself murdered the youth at

Rouen during April 1203, weighting the body of his nephew with a heavy stone before casting it into the river. If this is true it was a bad omen because from that moment John began to lose a war he had once looked like winning. Within a year the whole of Normandy was lost; except for the Channel Islands which still hold the unique consequence of being independent of the British Parliament but yet owing a personal loyalty to the British sovereign.

For a time there was a danger that England could be invaded and conquered all over again from a Normandy once more hostile to England. Yet as that danger receded another took its place.

The responsibility for appointing bishops had never been clear. In practice the king chose whom he wanted. The church went through the motions of choosing and invariably supported the king's original decision, which in turn was ratified by the Pope in Rome, who acted as if the selection was entirely his. It became a ritual dance which satisfied everyone—until, in 1205, Hubert Walter, the Archbishop of Canterbury and Chancellor of England, died and John chose John de Gray to succeed. For once, the church disagreed and favoured a certain Prior Reginald. As a compromise the Pope, Innocent III, decided to appoint Stephen Langton, a man accepted neither by King John nor the church. When the Pope became convinced his authority was being defied, he sentenced the whole English church to an interdict; the banning of all church services and activities other than baptism of children and hearing confessions from the dying. John, supported by church and people, remained stubborn and for six years churches remained virtually closed on orders from Rome, until, in 1213, the Pope played his final trump card and excommunicated John—in effect denying the king access to God. So, after all, not only did King John now have to accept Langton as the new archbishop but he was forced to recognise, publicly, the Pope as his lord and master on earth. At Dover, he knelt at the feet of Pope Innocent's representative, symbolically surrendered his crown, and just as symbolically accepted its return. King John thus acknowledged that he was as subservient to the Pope as the lowliest peasant was to his lord.

Neither the barons nor the church approved of King John's

abject submission and their discontent grew with the King's ever higher tax demands to pay for his new wars on the continent. A consequence of John's submission was that in return the Pope promised to persuade the Holy Roman Emperor to support John if the king decided to fight again for his lost territory in Normandy and Aquitaine. Thus tempted, the king tried unsuccessfully throughout 1213 and 1214 to regain his continental inheritance, but to no-one's surprise he and his ally, the Holy Roman Emperor, were convincingly defeated.

The barons of England, especially those in the north, decided enough was enough. Taxation and levies to support the king's continental wars were crippling the country's economy and the barons elected to march on London and demand an end to John's extravagance. As they marched south other groups, merchants, traders, and city-dwelling craftsmen joined the mass protest, each section of the community adding their own demands to the petition they would present to the king. It was civil war in all but name, a rebellion that threatened to engulf those who remained loyal to the king.

After the death of William the Conqueror in 1087 when he, and he alone, commanded instant loyalty and respect from all his subjects, England had changed. Since the successive kings had loosened their autocratic hold on every facet of society, the early Norman lords had given way to hereditary earls and barons who considered themselves English with little or no ambition to recover the king's continental territories. The king no longer demanded knights actually to fight for him in person unless they wanted to, provided their lord paid a tax called 'scutage' with which the king recruited mercenaries to fight his wars abroad. The peasantry too had developed an appetite for freedom and justice since the Norman conquest, and more and more were becoming tenants rather than serfs. As yet the appetite was not being totally satisfied but the relationship between serf and tenant on the one hand and land-owning master on the other was gradually becoming relaxed. Even if living conditions for the lowest strata of society were still poor, this version of the feudal system was already several degrees better than the French and Spanish counterparts. The sturdy independence of the English character was beginning to surface and many chronicles of the time refer to the sense of fun and high spirits developing among the lower classes. Already they had begun to combine loyalty and obedience with a healthy disrespect for authority which would be the country's future strength. The descendants of this generation were to be the free patriotic yeoman who would in centuries to come serve Henry the Fifth at Agincourt and Wellington at Waterloo.

It was against this background that the barons gathered support as they approached London.

A short time earlier King John had recognised the importance of London and had granted certain freedoms to the city in the form of a charter, including the right to elect a mayor who would represent the citizens. As a concession it achieved nothing. The City of London added still further demands onto the lengthening petition.

Early in June, 1215, King John rode a few miles east from his castle at Windsor and came face to face with his barons assembled in a meadow close to the River Thames at Runnymede. Here the barons presented their long petition, a document recognised as perhaps the most important in English History: Magna Carta or, in modern English, 'The Great Charter'.

The document had swollen to 63 clauses or conditions and King John agreed to them all, except one which aimed to exclude the City of London from taxation and the king saw this as too dangerous a precedent to accept. Two clauses in particular must be quoted in full simply because without them Magna Carta might now be forgotten and totally irrelevant. Clause 39: No Freeman shall be taken or imprisoned or outlawed or banished or in any ways destroyed, nor will we pass upon him, nor will we send upon him, unless by lawful judgement of his peers, or by law of the land. Clause 40: We will sell to no man, we will not deny to any man, either justice or right.

Other clauses dealt with the administration of justice, payment of debts, safe conduct of merchants, legality of standard weights and measures and the freedom to travel abroad freely. Nevertheless, it is clause 39, which protected men from being thrown into prison indefinitely without first being brought to trial, which is so important. We call it *Habeus Corpus* (deliver the body) and its provisions are widely quoted by lawyers today.

It might be a mistake to overestimate the importance of *Magna Carta*. The document ignored serfs and peasants who did not own land, it never became incorporated into law and there was no parliament in 1215 to ensure every condition was maintained; this task was delegated to a sub-committee of four barons. Some future generations chose to ignore *Magna Carta* and many more were in supreme ignorance of its existance. When, for example, in 1596 Shakespeare wrote his play *King John* he made no mention of *Magna Carta*.

The document has no known author and there is no attempt to disguise its blunt demands with soft words. It is a rag-bag of rights and conditions that are precise, definite and almost incapable of ambiguity by legal trickery. For the first time an English king was constrained by his own subjects, and from *Magna Carta* there could be no turning back. The principle of no man, not even the king, considering himself above the law of the land had been established. It was only the beginning of a crude form of democracy but it was a beginning.

The Church, prompted by the Pope's disapproval, repudiated *Magna Carta* and were reminded that Pope Innocent III regarded any king of England merely as his vassal without authority to grant such conditions without approval from Rome. King John accepted the Pope's dictum and found himself again in direct opposition to his barons, who this time had an ally in King Louis of France, who landed an army in southern England unopposed.

King John was close to despair as he hurried south to meet the crisis. During October 1216 he crossed that watery indentation on England's mid-eastern coast, The Wash, and lost all his possession including all the royal treasure. As schoolboys have said ever since; 'King John lost his washing in The Wash'. The king was now 49 years old, about five feet five inches tall, and, after a lifetime of self-indulgent eating habits, was in poor health. It is recorded that soon after losing his treasure chest he dined on over-ripe peaches and a surfeit of apple-cider, contracting dysentry, and died at Newark. By his own wishes he was taken to Worcester and buried in the cathedral.

John was no saint; nevertheless he could claim to be unlucky. The causes of his undoing were the wars in Normandy and Aquitaine, probably unwinnable anyway with the odds so heavily against him, and finding himself faced by a Pope who not only opposed and humbled him but who also tempted him with further continental adventures when his real duty should have been to remain in England. Even so, *Magna Carta* was a landmark, and the administrative framework of government during John's reign stayed intact and strong enough for his ministers to keep the country united during his son's childhood as England's new king.

3

THE BIRTH OF PARLIAMENT (1216 to 1327)

On 28th October 1216 John's eldest son, a boy only nine years old was crowned King Henry the Third. For the next ten years he grew to manhood and watched his father's chief minister, Hubert de Burgh, give a demonstration of how a kingdom should be governed. Without too much trouble Hubert de Burgh expelled the French who had been occupying England's southern counties. He implemented *Magna Carta* and by stringent economies and a policy of taxation by consent he partially restored England's prosperity. Not surprisingly, Hubert de Burgh became a popular hero and aroused the jealousy of barons and young king alike.

In 1227 Henry reached the age when he could exercise the power of kingship, and a few years after that not only dismissed Hubert de Burgh but imprisoned him in the Tower of London. He subsequently escaped to popular acclaim and much rejoicing. Without Hubert de Burgh's restraining influence, King Henry now began to mismanage the country's affairs.

Having no regard for his own thin resources he started to patronise the arts. As a boy he had watched Salisbury and Lincoln Cathedrals rise in the new and exciting gothic style, and King Henry actively encouraged many fine buildings that have graced England's heritage ever since; including the rebuilding, begun in 1245, of our present Westminster Abbey. Adding further extravagance was Eleanor, his French-born wife from Provence, who shared her husband's taste for good food, wine, expensive tapestries, and fine clothes, and she brought her entire family with her to England so that they too could share the king's liberal hospitality.

As if all this was not sufficient drain on the country's resources,

Henry raised an army of mercenaries to seize Normandy and his lost continental territories. He failed so ignominiously that by the treaty of 1254 the only part left of his grandfather's great empire was Gascony; a small consolation being that this included the wine-growing districts of Bordeaux.

Henry the Third's sheer incompetence led, almost inevitably, to another rebellion by a combination of land-owning barons and city-dwelling merchants and burghers. Unlike the occasion preceding *Magna Carta* in 1215 the barons now had a leader, a strong-willed character who was as unscrupulous as King Henry. This man was Simon de Montfort and he was destined to play an important part in the future of England.

Simon de Montfort was a Frenchman who inherited land in England and also the title of Earl of Leicester. He married King Henry's sister, Eleanor, and, using his position close to the royal household, he manoeuvered the king to a meeting not at Runnymede but at Oxford. The old Witan of Edward the Confessor's days had gradually been institutionalised into a council of bishops and noblemen who advised in governing the country; a system that had worked very well in spite of the misrule of some monarchs. Simon de Montfort compelled King Henry to form a council drawn from twelve members of the King's Council and twelve to be nominated by the barons. This new Council of Twenty-Four would be entrusted to draft a constitution reducing the king's exercise of power. Knights from the outlying shires, and city merchants, would be appointed to supervise the implementation of the new constitution which was more radical than *Magna Carta*, and King Henry agreed to the proposal only under threats and pressure.

As in 1215, the Pope forced the king into a repudiation and again King Louis of France prepared to land in England and prevent the Oxford Council being formed. Such a Council, if copied on the continent, would spell the end of monarchy, autocratic rule, and it might even sweep away the feudal system itself. King Henry had no alternative but to prepare himself and his supporters for a full scale civil war. However, unlike the baron's revolt of 1215, the king had a loyal and trustworthy supporter: his son Edward, named in honour of Edward the

Confessor revered as England's patron saint.

Prince Edward was nineteen years old, six feet tall, and growing into manhood with a physique that impressed and inspired the royalist party who might otherwise have become disenchanted with King Henry's conduct. One of the Prince's nicknames was 'Longshanks' and indeed the length of his arm was taken as the measurement of the yard we still use today. The young Prince Edward had a reputation for being delinquent but as a man he accepted responsibility with a loyalty towards his father unknown in earlier generations of Plantagenets. As a Christian he never lost his faith and althouth in battle he fought hard and ruthlessly, he had a natural chivalry and a desire to be fair and just. Even while still young he showed every indication of becoming a truly great king. Now he encouraged his father to fight and to resist any demands made by rebellious barons.

After a number of skirmishes King Henry and Prince Edward met Simon de Montfort in battle on 14th May 1264 at Lewes in the county of Sussex, some forty miles due south of London. De Montfort's army comprised citizens of London and other urban boroughs, whilst the royalists were stiffened by mercenaries whose fighting qualities proved to be unreliable. Edward fought well and his sector was largely successful but his father was less able and as a result both were taken prisoner.

Simon de Montfort was now king in all but name and the following year, in January 1265, he called for a Great Council to meet at Westminster; every shire and town were asked to send two representatives and this assembly would discuss England's future. Many now regard this council as the birth of our House of Commons if not the advent of parliament itself. In truth this 'parliament' (the word is old-French and the 19th century writer Thomas Carlyle translated this as 'talking shop') achieved nothing positive and within a short time Simon de Montfort felt himself somewhat insecure as England's temporary ruler.

Queen Eleanor and her supporters were threatening to invade from France and one of de Montfort's most powerful and loyal friends, Roger Mortimer, was among many who were having second thoughts at such sweeping constitutional reforms. The idea of England without an effective king did not appeal to every rebellious baron and Mortimer had no difficulty in releasing Edward from captivity.

Simon de Montfort still held the king, whom he compelled to ride side by side with him, giving the impression that Simon and King Henry were acting together in unison. With the king unwillingly at his side Simon de Montfort fought the decisive battle against Prince Edward on 4th August 1265. By the River Severn at Evesham, in the English west-Midlands, Prince Edward and his growing band of enthusiastic supporters emerged utterly victorious when de Montfort was killed.

King Henry was duly released and continued to rule nominally as king in a reign that was extended to fifty-six years before he died at Westminster in November 1272. Nominally, because Edward, with his father's consent and gratitude, took more and more responsibility and as a conciliatory gesture *Magna Carta* was reactivated without the barons demanding it. Between 1265 and 1272 England resumed a life of peaceful tranquility, with neither harsh taxation nor rebellious elements to ruffle the surface. Prince Edward deserves much credit for this stability and he felt confident enough to travel abroad and take part in the Holy Land crusades. When he heard news of his father's death he saw no compelling reason to hurry home, indeed he did not return for another two years, taking an early opportunity to pay homage to the king of France and inspect his territory of Gascony.

King Edward the First proved to be a giant among early English kings, and not only in his physical appearance. His wisdom and sure-footedness in all he did manifested itself at once. Whilst quietly rejecting some unwelcome clauses in *Magna Carta*, he nevertheless took a gigantic step forward in 1275 by inviting every country shire and each city borough to send two representatives to attend a meeting of the resurrected Great Council.

The Parliament envisaged by Simon de Montfort thus entered English life quietly, almost surreptitiously. It happened so naturally that it caused little adverse comment from the Pope, nor from King Louis of France who regarded such democratic steps as an abdication of kingship. So who takes the credit for the creation of Parliament, with hereditary land-owning noblemen and senior bishops forming the House of Peers, and elected representatives from the shires and cities comprising the House of Commons? Did England make Parliament or, much nearer reality, did Parliament make England? This unique form of power-sharing was far ahead of its time, and has been the model for sound democratic government ever since. From this moment the king could rule only with the consent of his people as represented by Parliament and yet this consent made it easier for taxes to be collected and difficult decisions to be taken jointly by king and people together.

Our modern degree of sophistication and election of representatives did not happen overnight and on many occasions in the future an unwise king would flout good advice, taking advantage of a sovereign's power to dissolve and inaugurate Parliament at will. Some kings either ignored Parliament or ensured its members were tame royalists and, although its effectiveness has varied from century to century, Simon de Montfort and King Edward the First led the way towards a constitutional monarchy and democracy.

Apart from an occasional minor skirmish, King Edward turned his back on expensive continental adventures to win back Normandy. Instead, he decided to take advantage of the disputes between Welsh princes to annex Wales and incorporate it into the English orbit. In this he succeeded brilliantly by a combination of diplomacy and force of arms; at one stage he arranged for Simon de Montfort's daughter to marry Llewelwyn, one of the Welsh princes, and then later executed that same Llewelwyn's brother when this, too, was to his advantage. Edward was skilful enough to subjugate Wales without destroying the Welsh culture, customs or language, all of which still survive today. What he did do was absorb the tribal customs into a modified feudal system and Anglicise the administration into shires. At the same time he retained the same border between England and Wales so that each country would keep its own identity.

By a happy coincidence the king's first son to survive infancy, also to be called Edward, was born during 1284 in Wales, at Caernarvon Castle and in 1301 he was officially given the title Prince of Wales.

All eldest sons of the monarchy have enjoyed this name ever

since. There is, alas, no truth in the story of the young Edward being shown to the townspeople of Caernarvon as an infant and presented as the Prince of Wales at his birth. This fable joins that of Blondel's serenading and Robin Hood as good stories unsupported by hard facts.

Like his father Henry the Third, King Edward enjoyed a most happy relationship with his wife. Queen Eleanor travelled with her husband Edward everywhere, and she was once heard to declare that the distance from any point on earth to heaven was just the same so it mattered little where she actually died. In fact she died at Harby, near Nottingham, in 1290, and her body was brought to Westminster in twelve daily stages before a state funeral took place in Westminster Abbey. At each of these twelve stages a stone cross was later erected and three of the original crosses survive to this day. The final resting place was in the village of Charing close to Westminster and when a cross was erected there, the village was renamed Charing Cross.

Having successfully dealt with Wales, King Edward now turned his attention to Scotland, again taking advantage of internal disputes. Since the days of Henry the Second, most of Scotland's border region and lowlands had been in English hands and now Edward struck further north towards the highlands. Two worthy opponents arose to challenge King Edward and both gave the king considerable trouble.

William Wallace was the first. He fought bravely until his defeat at Falkirk in 1298 and after surviving as an outlaw, with no safe refuge for seven years, he was betrayed to the English, brought to London in chains and suffered a tortured execution at Smithfield, close to the City of London walls.

Robert the Bruce was the most persistant and, ultimately, the most successful. He led the defiant Scots with skill and cunning over the rough terrain he knew so well, supported by an overwhelming mass of Scottish people who had become bitterly resentful of a long English occupation. Edward's response to the uprising was uncharacteristically brutal and savage, hanging almost every member of Robert the Bruce's family when that warrior had suffered defeat and escaped to the far north. It was at this time that Robert the Bruce reputedly watched a spider spinning and respinning a web that constantly fell apart and he too resolved to 'try, try, and try again'.

At the time of his Scottish campaigning Edward the First was over fifty years old but as fit as any man half his age. In addition to the nickname 'Longshanks' he became known as 'Hammer of the Scots' and brought to London the famous stone on which Scottish kings sat to be crowned, building a coronation throne around the slab of stone so that henceforth his son and all future kings and queens could enjoy their coronations sitting indirectly on the Stone of Scone or, as the early Irish kings called it when it was *their* seat of coronation in Ireland, the Stone of Destiny. According to legend it was the stone that Jacob used to rest his head, when dreaming of the ladder to heaven.

In 1307 Robert the Bruce had become so inspired by the spider that he attacked the English forces with renewed strength. Although King Edward was ill, almost for the first time in his life, when he heard of Bruce's attack he insisted on rising from his sick bed and riding to Scotland. Before he could cross the border he died, at the age of sixty-eight, and he was buried in Westminster Abbey close to his father, Henry the Third, and his wife, Queen Eleanor.

During a lifetime of service to his kingdom Edward the First had secured the existence and continuation of Parliament, he had reformed further still the laws of England and extended the king's jurisdiction at the expense of local barons, whose interpretation of law could be unreliable. To his neighbours he was less kind, having annexed Wales and, for a time at least, subdued Scotland in a series of defeats that would have crushed any country but that.

If Edward the First was one of our very greatest kings, his son Edward the Second was one of our very worst. Everything the first Edward gained in Scotland, the second Edward lost. The first Edward had been manly, courageous and inspired respect, the second was weak, vain and homosexual. Edward the First had died on his way to do battle with a brave and honourable warrior, his son was destined to die dishonourably in a manner that historians have never found easy to describe. It is only fair to add that Edward the Second was physically strong, showed courage when jousting, and enjoyed hard manual labour as a recreation. Given the job of estate management he might have proved very capable but by temperament and personality he was quite unfit to rule England.

Taking his father's place to lead the English army against Robert the Bruce, he was initially successful although he relaxed, or perhaps lost interest, when the Scots had again been driven back into the highlands. Apologists for the new king might claim that the country was in debt and wars of attrition had become expensive. The fact is that Edward returned to England and continued his love-affair with Piers Gaveston, a young gentleman from France who exercised great influence over the young king, only twenty-three years of age at his accession. Gaveston's influence was mischievous rather than benign: he insulted many noblemen, he encouraged the king to take part in activities that were considered unmanly, he abrogated power unto himself and his reward was to destroy the people's initial goodwill towards their king and to earn the personal hatred of almost every man and woman he met. His conceit, arrogance, and indiscretions could only meet one conclusion in an age when violence and sudden death was commonplace.

A group of earls seized Piers Gaveston and used a contrived charge of illegal land-holding to give him a summary trial and swift execution. Furthermore, these same earls forced the broken-hearted king to give them high office as ministers and thus humble Edward to the point where he became an ineffective ruler of his kingdom.

As if on cue, Robert the Bruce now attacked again and overran many castles the English were holding inside Scotland. One such castle to be attacked was at Stirling, and although the garrison inside were surrounded, they did resist and the number of besieged soldiers obliged King Edward to attempt a rescue and lift the blockade. With a powerful force of 30,000 men (some later Scottish chronicles put the figure much higher) facing barely 9,000 Scots King Edward suffered the kind of beating that gives a military commander nightmares. Robert the Bruce forced the English to a defeat that was close to massacre and the place, only a few miles from Stirling, has given Scotsmen a word to fling in the teeth of Englishmen ever since Bannockburn. The date was Sunday 23rd June 1314.

For Bruce, Bannockburn was the victory which secured for him the throne of Scotland and an apparent independence for his new kingdom. He continued to sweep south and did not stop until he had occupied a fair proportion of northern England. For Edward, Bannockburn heralded a decline in his personal fortune from which he would not recover.

Soon after becoming king, Edward had married Isabel, daughter of the king of France. In spite of his homosexuality, Edward fathered four children, although in time Isabel came to despise her feckless husband. Her displeasure boiled over when Edward, after the trauma of Bannockburn, replaced the dead Gaveston with two new male favourites; Hugh Despencer and his son, also called Hugh. The earls, noblemen and barons rose in revolt after the disasters in Scotland, also protesting against Edward's association with the Despencers. In 1322 the rebel barons met the royalists in battle near a town called Boroughbridge in Yorkshire. Edward and the Despencers emerged victorious but the victory was short-lived. Queen Isabel was one of those women who were prepared to fight for power and the name by which Isabel is known to history—the 'She-Wolf of France'—seems particularly apt. The queen had become the mistress of Roger Mortimer—a descendant of the same Mortimer who had released Prince Edward before the Battle of Evesham in 1265. Isabel and Mortimer had been living together in France; now they returned and became the focal point for an overwhelming revolt and trial of strength against Edward. Both Despencers were hanged and the king imprisoned and forced to abdicate in favour of his eldest son, then a boy of fourteen and unaware of his father's corruption and who could reign only with the support of his mother and the ambitious Mortimer.

Later that same year, 1327, Edward found himself imprisoned in Berkeley Castle near Gloucester, some 150 miles west of London. There the king of England was murdered in a manner that was both disgusting and cowardly. His killers thrust a red-hot poker into his anus, mocking his sexual vices and, more importantly, leaving no external mark so that for a time he was thought to have died from natural causes. He was given a lavish, sumptuous, funeral by those who had conspired his death and their hypocrisy was so overwhelming that even six hundred years later its deception seems unbelievable.

This chapter has covered a period when the best and worst of English kingship was laid bare. It was a time of great building and progress in artistic achievement: the universities of Oxford and Cambridge became established and scientific benefits began to accrue. Roger Bacon's work on optics resulted in spectacles being worn, the works of Thomas Aquinas were discussed, and the frontiers of medical knowledge advanced. Music flourished as never before, and theatrical dramas received enthusiastic support from Edward the Second if not from his father. The thirteenth century was also a time in which the lower elements of society not only were less abused but could look forward to justice against those who offended: the machinery for government had been created, although Parliament had yet to assume form and purpose. City-merchants and land-owners alike had begun to profit from the trade in wool, which had been expanding throughout the century: Flanders and the Low Countries had become the principal export markets and the prosperity of this trade was now a major source of England's wealth.

The only event to disfigure this century was the persecution and expulsion of the Jews. Educated and ambitious, they made a successful living from money-lending, a trade always unpopular with those in debt. Measures to restrict Jewish trading practices became commonplace, even the widows and dependants of Jews found it legally impossible to recover debts: these were forfeit to the king. Stories and rumours of unchristian activities resulted in many false charges and consequent executions. In 1255, for example, eighteen Jews were hanged in Lincoln for the murder of a young boy, and later a further ninety were charged in London for the self-same crime. For a time Jews were forbidden to eat with gentiles and were required to wear a special triangular badge. In 1290, after much pressure from the Church, the Jews were finally expelled and were not allowed to return until the mid-seventeenth century.

4

England's new king, Edward the Third, even though only four-teen years old, spent the early years of his reign enduring a number of humiliations.

The first was to become aware that his father, Edward the Second, had been murdered and the killers were not only free but probably part of the royal court circle; fortunately for his peace of mind he remained in ignorance of his father's way of life and the manner of his death. Secondly, he was obliged to preside over a peace treaty with Scotland which even a teenage boy could see was shameful and insulting to the memory of his illustrious grandfather, King Edward the First. One condition of the treaty was that the king's young sister, Joan, be married to Robert the Bruce's four year old son, David. Another was that the famous coronation stone be returned to Scotland, and only the stubborn defiance of Westminster Abbey's abbot prevented it. A third humiliation, and perhaps the greatest, was to see his mother, Queen Isabel, committing adultery every day with the hated Mortimer; a man who seemed to be making all the decisions and overruling the King's Council whenever he wished; a man so loaded with honours and titles that his arrogance began to alienate every friend he ever had.

For three years King Edward accepted his situation, all the time growing in wisdom, experience, and developing a courage that was both moral and physical. Undoubtedly his development was helped by the wife he married at the age of sixteen; Phillipa of Hainault, a royal princess from Flanders. It proved to be a fortunate marriage that lasted for forty years, producing seven sons and five daughters: those who survived beyond infancy lived in unity and harmony, and if *their* descendants had shared this same goodwill the bloody encounters we call The Wars of the Roses need never have happened. However that was in the future and in 1330 King Edward had problems of the present.

Early in that year Edward, still only seventeen but already a father, organised a *coup d'etat* having Mortimer killed and his mother honourably banished to Castle Rising in Norfolk. He followed this by driving the Scots from northern England and making his border with Scotland secure from further attack. This gained the king almost immediate popularity and he proved his maturity by using the people's goodwill to advantage.

He began by deciding to rule only through parliament, regularly attending and consulting it on every possible occasion. It was Edward the Third who encouraged Parliament not merely to concern itself with the collection of taxes but to ensure those taxes were wisely spent, recognising that stringent controls to eliminate waste would be to his own advantage and make him new friends. For the first time English was spoken in our courts of law and this acknowledgement of the native language spread the fair administration of justice even wider, and was a major factor in unifying England into a nation. This new-found unity was put to the test in 1337 when once again an English king began to look across the channel towards France. Experience had shown that fighting the Scots had often been necessary but seldom profitable and the rich spoils of France had always been an irresistible temptation to English kings as they struggled to maintain or regain the provinces of Normandy, Anjou or Aquitaine, although the high cost of such enterprises had usually precipitated rebellion and dissent in England. However, in 1337 when King Edward began his conflict with France, loosely known as the Hundred Years War because it continued on and off until 1453, the circumstances were very different.

Since the Norman Conquest English kings had claimed the province of Normandy as of right, to this they added Aquitaine, brought into English ownership by the marriage of Henry the Second to Eleanor of Aquitaine, and the whole region of Anjou resulting from Matilda's marriage with Geoffrey Plantagenet, Count of Anjou. That some of these territories had already been lost in battle against the kings of France did not alter the essential right of title or ownership. The point at issue was: did the English kings hold the territory as a sovereign state in their capacity as a king of England, or was the king in the same subservient position to the French kings as the English land-owning barons were to *him*? Some English kings—Edward the First for example—did pay homage to their counterparts in France, others did not. In truth the matter was not always vital because, whilst some generations of both royal houses fought each other and some inter-married, they all regarded themselves as equal in rank.

When King Charles IV of France died, leaving no direct male heir, Edward's mother, Isabel, Charles' sister, should have been the natural successor and her son, Edward the Third, declared king of France and England. Unfortunately France recognised the Salic Law which excluded females from the line of succession so that the nearest male heir, Duke Philip of Anjou, became King Philip of France and he at once goaded and antagonised King Edward by positioning a French naval fleet off the coast of Flanders, denying England her lucrative trade in wool, and seizing Gascony the last French province in English hands. Edward was faced either with accepting Philip, whom he regarded as no more than a duke masquerading as a king, as his continental overlord or claiming the throne of France as his natural inheritance. He chose to fight, and so began The Hundred Years War. He even incorporated the *fleur de lys* into the royal coat of arms, where it remained until 1802 by which time the idea of our English king ruling France had long ago been abandoned. Parliament supported him in the coming war with enthusiasm, if only to maintain the export trade in wool. By brilliant seamanship, and effective use of the longbow at sea, Edward destroyed the French navel force at Sluys, near Antwerp, re-opening the trade with Flanders and paving the way for an invasion of France.

King Edward's eldest son, also called Edward but better known to history as the Black Prince, was only sixteen years old in 1346 yet he led the king's army into a battle near a village called Crècy. Whether he gained his name because of a black cloak he wore, or because of his black temper has been a subject for debate among historians ever since. Ill-temper or not he fought bravely, with intelligence, and used England's secret weapon to great advantage: this was the longbow. The strong flexible wood was usually yew or maple and each bow stood almost as high as the man using it. It had three main advantages over the mechanical cross-bow used by the French: it had a range twice that of the cross-bow; it was more accurate, piercing a knight's chain-mail with ease, and with experience a nimble-fingered archer fired more than double the arrows of his French counterpart. Furthermore, a greatly relaxed feudal system, and a feeling that his king's respect for law and justice protected him, encouraged every soldier to be loyal and proud of his country. The gulf between an English peasant or yeoman, and his lord, was narrowing and Crècy proved that each had respect for the other.

Not so the French. The richly clothed knights on their fine horses despised their own rank and file archers, and it was not unknown for French knights to ride over and through their own infantry in order to indulge themselves in an orgy of hand-to-hand combat.

At Crècy, in mid-August 1346, the English archers defeated a numerically superior force and even without the use of cannon and gunpowder—one of the earliest occasions when such weapons were known to be deployed—the victory was conclusive. King John of Bohemia, although totally blind, fought on the French side and was killed. His badge of three ostrich feathers and his motto 'Ich dien' (I serve) were adopted by the Black Prince and have remained the badge and motto of our Princes of Wales ever since.

Two years later Calais itself was beseiged and captured by the English. This was the occasion, illustrated by Rodin's statue which stands near the Houses of Parliament, with an identical one in Calais, when six burghers from the town surrendered with ropes round their necks and offered themselves for execution if the king would spare everyone else. Queen Phillipa pleaded on their behalf and they were saved.

We owe much of our knowledge of this period to Jean Froissart who faithfully chronicled Edward the Third's great battles, and whose records of the king's desire for chivalry have been proved to be the most honest and accurate accounts of that

time. This was The Age of Chivalry when women could expect to
be treated with honour, when enemies would fight hard but
according to rules of combat which protected the defenceless,
when prisoners of war were respected and stimulated a lucrative
trade in ransoms. King Edward the Third greatly admired the
ideals of chivalry and in 1348 created an exclusive order that is as
highly prized now as it was then: The Most Noble Order of
the Garter, with its spiritual home in St George's Chapel, at
Windsor Castle. The story of its foundation is romantic but well-
founded. After the defeat of Calais the king celebrated with a
lavish ball, and whilst dancing with an attractive lady, the
Countess of Salisbury, he noticed her blue garter had slipped
down her leg to the floor. To prevent the attendant knights
speculating why the garter had become loose the king placed the
garter on *his* leg and declared: '*Honi soit qui mal y pense*' (Evil be to
those who see evil). The blue garter, inscribed with the motto in
old-French, is still worn on special occasions by present-day
Knights of the Garter.

Edward the Third was so inspired by the ideals of chivalry and
the legends of King Arthur's knights that he ordered a round
table made to fit the Round Tower of Windsor Castle. The
notions of chivalrous conduct certainly were in evidence even
though they were not always achieved: battles fought with axes,
clubs, and swords were still messy, bloody and painful exper-
iences.

In 1356 another great victory was recorded, this time at
Poitiers, and the French king taken prisoner. King Edward the
Third was now recognised as the undisputed ruler of Gascony,
Aquitaine and Calais. In return for a huge ransom the King of
France was released and Edward withdrew his claim to the French
throne. King Edward had reached the height of his power and
popularity with the English people, and his stunning victories had
made the country rich. At this high-water mark in England's
history, disaster struck in the form of a calamity that was
unforeseen and against which there was no defence.

Spreading from central Asia came a type of bubonic plague so
virulent that it threatened to destroy mankind: the Black Death.
It reduced the population of England from four million to two

and a half million in less than fifty years. At the time it seemed
like a judgement of God, the end of the world, as there were
three separate waves of the disease; in 1349, 1362 and 1369. Many
of those who survived remained weak, incapable of procreation,
or simply too crippled to be of use. With the labour force thus
depleted it was not long before England's economy began to
suffer; work on many great cathedrals and abbeys came to a
standstill, fields were untilled and livestock neglected.

In spite of the Black Death and the peace treaty with France
some fighting continued, with the Black Prince scoring a number
of inconclusive victories. Against Scotland King Edward succeeded
in occupying the lowlands again and yet the early glories of his
reign were gone. The sun began to set all too quickly and the
king drifted into a period of premature senility.

Queen Phillipa, the king's strength and inspiration, died in 1369
and he fell into the hands of Alice Perrers who simply took
advantage of a man in physical and mental decline. Unlike Henry
the Third, who also went into an early decline, Edward had no
son strong enough to accept responsibility. The Black Prince,
England's great hope for the future, contracted dropsy and
became a mere shadow until his merciful death in 1376. All the
king's other sons were too involved in their own affairs to
concern themselves nationally, even John of Gaunt (so-called
because he was born in Ghent, near Antwerp), the most cultured,
educated and attractive of men had built himself a position of
influence and wealth that was satisfying enough in itself; he
remained content to protect his own interests, offering advice
only when it was asked for. By patronising Chaucer and many
other writers, artists, builders and philosophers John of Gaunt
made a major contribution to England's heritage, at the same
time recognising the Black Prince's young son, Richard, as the
undisputed heir.

On 21st June 1377 King Edward the Third died, alone except for
Alice Perrers who reputedly stripped the rings from his body. He
had reigned for fifty years and seen the country emerge victorious
from every military campaign. The Black Death had been a set-
back but England was at last a nation promising to emerge
economically strong and with a culture including literature

written in a common language now spoken by all the people high and low.

King Richard the Second was just ten years of age when the death of his father and grandfather catapulted him into an early kingship. Even at that age Richard showed an enterprise and intelligence which benefitted from the experience of his uncle, John of Gaunt. Only four years later, at the age of fourteen, Richard was faced with a crisis that might have troubled any king in any age but the youth proved himself a real leader and stamped his own authority on men twice his age and more. The crisis was the Peasants' Revolt of 1381.

One consequence of the Black Death and its dramatic reduction of the labour force was the collapse of the feudal system as workers found themselves in demand, commanding wages and freedom based on their increased value. John of Gaunt, acting as Regent for the newly-crowned boy-king had tried to control wages by statute and this led directly to peasants physically rebelling against their masters.

The revolt began in Kent, a richly agricultural county south-east of London, and Wat Tyler—a discontented soldier recently returned from the wars in France—became their leader as they marched to London. Near Greenwich they were joined by rebels from other parts of England and a rabble-rousing priest called John Ball further inflamed them with his radical ideas. Liberal religious doctrine attacking the church's wealth was much in fashion and John Ball skilfully combined his complaints with that of the peasants. He coined the enigmatic rhyme which other, later, rebels would also declaim: 'When Adam delved and Eve span, Who was then the gentleman?' It could have been put much more simply by asserting that in the beginning everyone was equal.

Led by Wat Tyler the mob entered London, killing and terrorising priests, religious leaders, and the lawyers who were now a fast-growing profession. Young King Richard met Wat Tyler, deviously agreed to discuss his grievances inside the city and laid a trap so that the Lord Mayor of London, in person, stabbed Wat Tyler to death; the flag of the City of London has had a dagger in the top left hand corner ever since. With Wat Tyler dead the rebellion disintegrated and Richard hanged as many ringleaders as he could find. The fact that a fourteen year old boy had faced the rebels and outwitted them was not lost on the people, nor was Richard himself unaware of his growing prestige.

As king, Richard the Second disagreed with sharing power and he decided to ignore Parliament and rule as an autocrat, making his own decisions with a minimum of consultation. One result was a conscious effort not to pursue any further wars in France. His reason told him such wars were unprofitable regardless of which side won or lost. Instead he emulated his uncle, John of Gaunt, and resumed the great building programme interrupted by the Black Death. It was Richard who was responsible for the completion of Westminster Abbey and his portrait—the first true likeness of any English king—greets the present-day visitor as he enters the nave. It was Richard who civilised the court, formalised etiquette and gentlemanly behaviour, and who invented the pocket handkerchief as an alternative to wiping his nose on a coat sleeve.

Richard had married a lady from the country we now call Czechoslovakia, Anne of Bohemia, and although this was most certainly a love-match they produced no children. Her death in 1394 affected Richard's hitherto sound judgement and from the time of her death his position became weaker as he drifted into an isolation and solitude unbroken by a second marriage.

His intellect and independent attitude did not make him popular and the climax of his unpopularity came when John of Gaunt—who had added the title Duke of Lancaster to his other names—died and Richard, deciding such power and influence constituted a virtual state-within-a-state, appropriated much of it into his own hands. John of Gaunt's son Henry Bolingbroke had already quarrelled with Richard and been banished from England. He now returned, angry and resentful. He claimed the throne for himself and forced Richard aside; a clumsy usurpment that created a deadly precedent for his own descendants. A year later, in 1400, Richard was cruelly murdered in Pontefract Castle by which time Henry Bolingbroke had already been crowned King Henry the Fourth.

When Henry the Fourth usurped King Richard it was a signal

that the civilised way of making changes had been abandoned, that law and order counted for nothing when faced with an unashamedly naked lust for power. Parliament, led by discontented earls and barons were eager for change, as the autocracy of Richard had not been to their taste. Nevertheless, once the forces of murder, intrigue and opportunism are unleashed everyone is in danger.

The Wars of the Roses, a long confusing civil war to decide the line of succession, started in 1455, although it is significant that Shakespeare's magnificent pageant of historical plays covering these wars begin earlier, with Richard the Second being displaced by his cousin, Henry. This is a point to remember when we consider the short reign of Henry the Fourth which lasted from 1399 to 1413, a reign punctuated by minor rebellions of earls and barons who were greedy, jealous of each other, and considered themselves poorly rewarded for supporting Henry's seizure of power. The cultivation of art, music and architecture stopped and religious persecution began to deface England. It was a time of misery, misgovernment and institutionalised law-breaking. Even the Welsh, so long quiet and peaceful, tried to take advantage and secure their old freedom. Owain Glyndwr was the brave unselfish Welshman who tried but failed to create an independant Wales, and it is sad to see this noble warrior so caricatured as Owen Glendower in Shakespeare's play of Henry IV. The spluttering insignificant revolts continued until the king's death in 1413; indeed the manner of his death is probably remembered more than his disordered life.

It had been prophesied that he would die in Jerusalem and he eagerly looked forward to a Holy Land crusade and the possibility of his own martyrdom there. Instead, early in 1413, he made a routine visit to Westminster Abbey and was there attacked by a seizure of the heart. He was carried into the abbot's lodging and died in the room that bears the same name now as it did before the king's birth; the Jerusalem Chamber.

So much of our feeling towards Henry the Fourth's son, another Henry, Henry the Fifth, has been coloured by Shakespeare's play of the same name. There is little evidence that as a young man, Prince Hal enjoyed riotous living in the taverns and inns, drinking the nights away with low-born braggarts and women of ill-repute. In fact much of his youth was spent fighting the Welsh rebels and studying at Queen's College, Oxford. Nor was he quite the chivalrous soldier as portrayed on stage or screen; at Rouen, for example, during his wars in France, he allowed almost fifty thousand women, children and old men to die of cold and starvation when a little old-fashioned chivalry might have saved them. On an earlier occasion he watched a young blacksmith being burned to death as a heretic—he had denied that the sacrament of bread and wine was truly Christ's body—and Henry ordered the fire to be put out and the man given an opportunity to recant. When the man refused, Henry ordered the fire relit and stayed to see the poor wretch burned alive. On the other hand he cared about the poor and needy of his own country and many documents of the time are littered with his personal comments recommending clemency and charity.

Born in 1387, he lived in an age of complicated personalities and Henry the Fifth remains a mass of contradictions. He was intelligent, and had a great love of music and poetry. He was humane enough to take Richard the Second's body from its lowly grave outside London, where it had been buried without ceremony by his father Henry the Fourth, and place him reverently beside Anne of Bohemia in Westminster Abbey. Even so, Henry the Fifth's reputation rests on his career as a great soldier, an inspiring leader, and above all on one battle that has fired the imagination of every generation since. Agincourt.

The very name summons up a picture of valiant knights, hand to hand combat, sun glinting on swords as horses thundered towards each other in a mighty clash of arms. That such hard won gains were thrown away by the next generation and Henry's unsoldierly son only adds to the drama and the sheer glorious pointlessness of such battles.

Since the great victories of Crècy, Poitiers and Calais, fought by Edward the Third and his son the Black Prince, France had quietly regained much of her lost territories and Henry the Fifth decided to claim the French crown when the King of France refused to settle their differences by personal combat. Parliament and people united behind the king and long careful preparations were made before the invasion. The lure of plunder, booty and prisoners' ransom brought volunteers rushing to take part, and in mid-October 1415 the army landed in France.

In spite of all the planning it was soon discovered that supplies of rations would be insufficient for Henry's army, and the countryside in October could not provide the amount of food necessary. An epidemic of dysentry did not help, neither did the incessant rain, nor was morale raised when the French declined to stand and fight. King Henry saw his chance of any sort of victory ebbing away as he turned his army back towards Calais, dispirited and hungry. Then fate took a hand as it so often does on battlefields.

The French sensed the poor state of Henry's army and they despatched a herald to tell the English king that a site had been chosen for the battle; a large field sown with corn, roughly two miles long and one mile wide, with woods sheltering it from the nearest village, Agincourt. Henry's army numbered 6,000 and the French 20,000. Seeing the odds against him King Henry offered to vacate the battlefield, pay for any damage done by his marching army, and return to England. Not surprisingly the French refused the chance of foregoing such an easy victory and prepared to revenge themselves for Crècy and Poitiers. Henry the Fifth inspired his army, and no doubt himself, by wearing in his battle-helmet the huge ruby once owned by the Black Prince (miraculously it survived and now adorns the Imperial State Crown worn by our sovereigns on all state occasions), with the result that Agincourt was one of the greatest victories won on any battlefield at any time.

Since Crècy the French had learned nothing. As then, their proud haughty knights crashed headlong into the swarm of English arrows, and still wearing their heavy armour impaled themselves on sharpened staves sunk into soft earth to protect the English archers. Now Henry and his mounted knights attacked the disorganised French and the pile of dead rose even higher: 7,000 Frenchmen were killed and the very highest number of English dead was said to be less than 250. The words 'victory' or 'defeat' have no meaning in such circumstances. In one afternoon the flower of French nobility lay dead or dying, and the French king's son captured and held for ransom. However the war was not yet won.

To conquer France entirely Henry had to beseige one fortified town after another. At this period of military history all the odds were in favour of the defenders who frequently were better supplied, fed and housed than the army camping uncomfortably beneath the city walls. Slowly, however, one town after another was captured, including Rouen with the inhuman killing of its inhabitants mentioned earlier.

Eventually the French, the majority of their knights already slain at Agincourt, accepted defeat and although Henry the Fifth was not himself declared King of France it was agreed that Henry's heirs and successors should be so crowned when the present king, Charles VI, died. To seal all that had been agreed, Henry married the king's daughter, Princess Katherine of Valois. The two warring countries were now united by treaty and marriage and it must have seemed to everyone at that time that an everlasting peace had been achieved.

King Henry the Fifth and his new bride, Queen Katherine as she now was, returned to a series of grand celebrations in England. Never, perhaps, in our entire history, has one king been so universally feted and applauded.

In triumph he returned to France to complete the conquest of those stubborn provinces that had remained hostile, until on 31st August 1422, at the age of thirty-five, he died near the castle of Vincennes in France.

His funeral in Westminster Abbey was an affair of rich ceremony and genuine grief, his final resting place being in the shrine, close to that of the abbey's founder, Edward the Confessor.

Ironically King Charles of France died only a few days after Henry the Fifth, and his death immediately invoked the treaty signed by both kings. So, at the age of nine months, King Henry's son and heir, yet another Henry, the sixth English king to bear that name, was proclaimed King of France and King of England.

With only a baby to reign in such troubled times England was set on a course that was beyond both prophesy and imagination.

5

Until he was five years old King Henry the Sixth was cared for by his widowed mother, Queen Katherine. She was then obliged to leave the court after the scandal of having married a junior member of her household, Owen Tudor. (It was their grandson, Henry Tudor, who was destined to be a king of England, Henry the Seventh.)

Richard Beauchamp, Earl of Warwick, now became the young king's tutor and responsible for moulding the boy's character. Kindliness, courtesy, compassion and a love of religious know-ledge were the qualities Henry carried into manhood. For a potential saint or holy man it was excellent training, and it is true that the people loved him, never seeking justice from him in vain, but his modesty and unworldliness allowed him merely to accept the buffets of fate and not control his own destiny. His passion for learning found expression in the founding of many schools and colleges. Before he was twenty years old All Souls College in Oxford had been established, also King's College at Cambridge, and, within the sight of Windsor Castle, Eton College, arguably the finest or at least the most famous school in England.

Meanwhile the kingdoms of France and England had to be governed in the king's name until Henry came of age. A number of earls and dukes jostled for power, forming alliances to propagate their own influence: the two main rivals were both royal dukes, brothers of the dead king and so uncles to Henry the Sixth.

John, Duke of Bedford, acted as the boy-king's Regent in France, negotiating with those who supported King Henry, fighting those who did not. He was a highly cultured man and several French universities owe their beginnings to him, he was also fond of music and patronised a number of composers, including the great John Dunstable.

Humphrey, Duke of Gloucester, the second uncle, was equally cultured although his abiding passion was books; it was his library which formed the basis of the Bodlian Library at Oxford University. Good Duke Humphrey, as he came to be known, left one other lasting memorial to his name although he could never have foreseen its modern claim to fame: he built a house on the riverside at Greenwich, a few miles downriver from Westminster, later to be demolished and provide the site for a great royal palace where Henry the Eighth and Elizabeth the First would be born. Later still the Royal Naval College and the largest maritime museum in the world would be built there, and on top of a local hill his octagonal watch-tower provided useful foundations on which the Greenwich Observatory and prime meridian line would appear, to give the modern world its present time scale. Good Duke Humphrey acted as the king's warden in England, which did not prevent him trying to interfere with his brother's responsibilities in France, where all the gains of Henry the Fifth were gradually being lost.

Some French provinces, like Gascony, preferred the English system of rule and justice, others like Burgundy preferred to be independent and only allied themselves with England to defeat, if they could, the French. Meanwhile many other provinces of France began to demand the end of England's occupation and the dispirited French aristocracy were suddenly aroused and inspired by the appearance of a seventeen year old country girl who convinced them that she had heard the voice of God and that the destiny of France was in her hands. She proved her point by forcing the English to lift their siege of Orleans and leading the French to a further victory at Patay. She was captured, not by the English but by soldiers from Burgundy, put on trial by the French as a witch, and burnt at the stake. At her death on 30th May 1431 Joan of Arc was just nineteen years old.

One observer at her trial was the ten year old Henry the Sixth who had been brought to France for his formal coronation in Paris as the King of France, the only English king to have the distinction of being crowned king of both countries. The ceremony was an illusion. Slowly the English in France were losing ground, lacking the support of men and money from England. In 1435 the Duke of Bedford died and with him went the last chance of holding back the French.

Good Duke Humphrey was soon in no position to take advantage of his brother's death and consolidate his own position close to the king, because his wife Eleanor was convicted of sorcery and imprisoned, the resultant scandal diminishing the duke's influence. A few years later he died in mysterious circumstances and it is generally accepted that he was murdered by those resentful of the position he still held within the court. Into this vacuum stepped a number of dukes and earls, but none of them with greater power than King Henry's new bride.

At the age of twenty-three, in 1445, Henry married Margaret of Anjou, sixteen years old and a French princess. As a goodwill gesture to France the king had relinquished the province of Maine but this only encouraged the French to further military advances; Henry's title of King of France becoming meaningless as the English army continued to retreat. This was bad enough yet it was Margaret's character which was the greater danger.

Of all the royal tigresses that have snarled and fought their way through history, Margaret of Anjou was probably the most unpleasant. She very quickly learned to despise her husband, picking quarrels and fighting with anyone and everyone who disagreed with her. It was Margaret who ensured that Henry's natural kindliness and ability to compromise were thwarted, so that even mild disagreements were magnified into confrontation. Not that the rebellion of 1450 could have been resolved by honeyed words.

King Henry's virtues of modesty and moral principles had no appeal for the discontented, unpaid, soldiers drifting back from France and led by Jack Cade they began to repeat Wat Tyler's revolt of 1381. Once again the open space near Greenwich, called Blackheath, was the place at which the rebellious mob assembled before marching to London. This time there was no brave Richard the Second to stand in their way and match them with cunning, and the mob attacked London and for a time controlled it. The rebellion eventually fizzled out, and Jack Cade and his ringleaders pursued and executed. Nevertheless, it was a serious, politically motivated, revolt and it was thought to have been inspired by Richard, Duke of York, the king's cousin.

Of Edward the Third's sons who survived to marry and produce children, his eldest was the Black Prince whose son had succeeded to the throne as Richard the Second. Edward the Third's second son, Lionel, Duke of Clarence, produced a daughter, and her grand-daughter, Anne, married Richard, Earl of Cambridge; he being in direct male descent from Edward the Third's fourth son, Edmund, Duke of York. This Earl of Cambridge was beheaded for treason in 1415 but his son, also called Richard and styled Duke of York, was the man now beginning to flex his muscles and stake a claim for the throne occupied by Henry the Sixth. The Duke of York could claim that in the female line he was descended from Edward the Third's *second* son, whereas Henry the Sixth descended from John of Gaunt, Duke of Lancaster, Edward the Third's *third* son. If, on the other hand, descent through the female line was inadmissable there was no disputing that Richard, Duke of York, was in direct male succession to his grandfather Edmund, fourth son of Edward the Third, and therefore had as much right to usurp Henry the Sixth as Henry Bolingbroke had to overthrow Richard the Second. On such issues would wars be fought and men die in their thousands.

At the time of Jack Cade's rebellion, Richard, Duke of York, did not, in public, justify his claim quite so forcibly as he did in private, but his supporters were beginning to consider him as potentially a better king than the weaker Henry the Sixth. They openly showed their anger and disappointment at the outcome of the Hundred Years War, which in 1453 ended with military defeat for England and the reduction of Henry's domain in France to the port of Calais and a small enclave surrounding it. All this coincided with a bout of insanity to which King Henry was prone, and Richard was authorised as Regent, king in all but name. By the time Henry had recovered and Richard returned power to him, Margaret of Anjou had produced a son who distanced Richard still further from an eventual lawful succession. This was the catalyst from which the ensuing conflict sprang.

The Wars of the Roses were given their romantic title only by later generations and no evidence exists to support Shakespeare's fiction, in Henry VI Part I, that the two rival leaders plucked a white and red rose as their emblems from the flowers of Temple Gardens in London. Certainly, the supporters of Richard, the Yorkists, displayed the White Rose of Yorkshire on their banners and crests, counterbalanced by the Red Rose of Lancashire to denote support for the king who was descended from John of Gaunt, Duke of Lancaster. Without doubt the series of conflicts scarcely merit the dignity of being described as 'wars'; they were little more than extended gang fights, the object being not to conquer territory nor change anyone's religion or way of life, but to slay or maim each other and determine which branch of the same family should provide the line of descent and be king. For all but professional historians or truly dedicated students, this period is the most confusing and complicated episode of English history. Noble families became involved, many changed sides according to their estimation of where the advantage lay, acts of betrayal were commonplace and the only fair comparisons are with the family feuds so prevalent in Sicily or the Chicago gangland of Al Capone. The great majority of the population could only watch their aristocratic betters kill each other, and marvel at the folly of what they saw.

They saw, during the spring of 1454, rival armies converging into the unwalled cathedral city of St Albans, some 20 miles north of London. Unlike Crécy or Agincourt both sides possessed archers of quality, and in the confined streets of St Albans they proved themselves deadly and effective. King Henry had set up his royal standard outside the Castle Inn near the market place, but he was soon taking refuge in the cathedral as the Yorkists gained the initiative. Richard Neville, Earl of Warwick, whose personal army was the largest and most decisive element ensured victory for Richard, Duke of York, who although he had won knelt at the king's feet, renewing his pledge of loyalty, and together the two men rode to London, surrounded by Yorkist soldiers. Richard, Duke of York, was appointed Constable of England, his victorious army 'forgiven' and peace returned for a time. Margaret of Anjou, however, could neither forgive nor forget, and under her tigerish influence the king and his Lancastrians recovered some of their confidence.

The powerful Earl of Warwick had gone to Calais to stiffen its defences against the encroaching French but he returned to England in 1459, allied himself with the Yorkists again, and prepared to fight. At Blore Heath the Yorkists were victorious; a few weeks later, at Ludlow, Margaret of Anjou dragooned the Lancastrians to success. The Yorkists regrouped and defeated the royalists with a victory at Northampton that seemed decisive, with the Earl of Warwick and his badge of a 'bear and ragged staff' (one of his ancestors had once killed a huge bear by using a heavy branch of tree as his club) again much in evidence. The Duke of York now openly sought the crown of England from Parliament but was refused, in spite of the Yorkists overwhelming display of military force.

Meanwhile Margaret of Anjou was reinforcing the Lancastrians in the north of England and seeking further support from England's old enemy, Scotland. Richard, Duke of York, decided to march north and attack, confident enough to leave the Earl of Warwick in London. It proved a poor miscalculation. Near Wakefield Richard was ambushed and killed, his head wreathed in a derisory crown of paper and exhibited on the city walls of York.

The dead duke's son, eighteen year old Edward, known as the Earl of March, now led the Yorkists and he it was who captured Owen Tudor, husband of Queen Katherine and grandfather of a future king of England, and executed him, an act that ensured the Tudor's enmity towards the Yorkists both present and future. Edward, Earl of March, and Richard Neville, Earl of Warwick, now marched to join each other until Margaret of Anjou intervened and attacked the Earl of Warwick in a second battle in St Albans. Margaret's ferocity won her a victory but she could not prevent the Yorkists from uniting into one strong army and marching to London.

It was now clear to everyone that King Henry the Sixth was a mere figurehead and his unpopular wife the true ruler. Perhaps for this reason the Earl of Warwick demanded that the dead Duke of York's son, Edward, should now be accepted as king, and he was. On 4th March 1461 England had a new king, Edward the Fourth, at six feet four inches he was, and still is, England's tallest king. Within a month he was facing Margaret of Anjou again; this time at Towton, a few miles south of York. It was to be the biggest and bloodiest battle to take place on English soil.

In the teeth of a blizzard the Yorkists and Lancastrians shot and hacked each other to death; King Edward the Fourth on one side, the deposed King Henry the Sixth on the other. Longbows, swords, axes, clubs and guns—of varying sizes and accuracy—were used by both armies with devastating effect. Reports of the dead counted after the battle are not unanimous but it is generally accepted that 28,000 bodies were found in the snow and mud. Some were foreign mercenaries being paid to fight, the rest were Englishmen killed by other Englishmen in a cause that was without principle and lacked any religious or ideological overtones.

Many Lancastrians fled to Scotland, together with Margaret, her husband and her son, whilst Edward returned in triumph for his coronation in Westminster Abbey on 21st June 1461, his younger brothers George, Duke of Clarence, and Richard, Duke of Gloucester sharing the honour and the glory.

Edward began the rebuilding of St George's Chapel in Windsor Castle, the one so familiar to us today, and for a time culture and the pursuit of learning returned. King Edward forgave many who had opposed him and a cheerful optimism began to pervade England again; always remembering the merchant classes were not involved in the wars and their trade to and from the continent was largely unaffected. The peace was temporary and illusory even though Henry the Sixth had allowed himself to be captured and was now safely out of sight in the Tower of London.

Richard Neville, Earl of Warwick, had gone to France and whilst there he heard that King Edward had married a woman five years older than himself, with two sons by an earlier marriage. Her name was Elizabeth Woodville and her family had been bitter rivals of the Warwicks for many years. The Earl of Warwick unashamedly craved power and influence and he now saw, quite accurately, that the new youthful king would not be a compliant puppet, not even to the earl who had been instrumen-

tal in putting him on the throne. For a time the earl remained
loyal until he made the decision to change sides, restore Henry to
the throne and regain that power and influence denied him by
King Edward.

Margaret of Anjou was in France with her son, Prince Edward
who in 1470 was thirteen years of age, and she agreed that the
youth should marry the Earl of Warwick's fifteen year old
daughter, Anne. For the earl, who could never be king himself,
this was as close as he could get, and if the price was allying
himself with his old adversary, Margaret of Anjou, then that price
would be paid; together they decided to invade England. Not for
nothing is the Earl of Warwick known to history as 'Warwick the
Kingmaker'.

The earl went to England first and immediately found support
from the Lancastrians as his ever-growing army marched on
London. They released King Henry and watched him crowned for
the second time. Edward the Fourth very quickly slipped away to
Flanders, returned again the next year, 1471, and prepared for
battle against his one-time champion the Earl of Warwick.
Margaret of Anjou, meanwhile, was preparing to land in the west
of England, gather support in Wales and unite with Warwick to
defeat Edward the Fourth.

Edward was no military genius and he was lucky to meet
Warwick on a dank misty day when mistaken identities added to
the confusion. The place was Barnet, on the northern edge of
modern London, the date was 14th April 1471; Easter Sunday.
Richard, Duke of Gloucester, only eighteen years old but fanatical-
ly loyal to his brother Edward, fought as hard as anyone and by a
combination of courage and confusion the Yorkists routed Warwick and his Lancastrians; the Earl of Warwick being killed when
a soldier found him wounded, lifted the earl's visor to identify
him and repeatedly stabbed a sword into the earl's head and face.

Edward and his brothers had no time to celebrate. Margaret of
Anjou had gathered an army together and at Tewksbury on the
River Severn—not far from Evesham where Simon de Montfort
had been defeated in 1265—the Yorkists and Lancastrians prepared to fight yet again. And again Edward was in luck. None of
the Lancastrian noblemen would allow Margaret to command

them in battle and she was banished to the nearby abbey for safe refuge. Edward found the Lancastrians divided and suspicious of each other, and supported by 200 men armed with spears he pushed and chased the opposition into the fast-flowing river; almost as many were drowned as died of wounds. Margaret's young son, Edward, so recently married, was killed and this demoralised her into a surrender she could hardly avoid.

King Henry the Sixth, his hopes dashed by the successive failures of Warwick and Margaret, was deposed for the second time and sometime during the night of Tuesday, 21st May 1471, was murdered by unknown hands in the Tower of London. A saintly, gentle, forgiving man of fifty he had been totally unsuited to be king of England. His wife, Margaret of Anjou, the cause of so much trouble fared better; she died eleven years later at the age of fifty-three, having been ransomed to King Louis of France.

Edward the Fourth was now undisputed king and the final ten years of his reign were little short of dazzling. He patronised every facet of the arts from musicians to artists and philosophers to poets; moreover it was during his reign that William Caxton introduced both a postal system and printing into England, so that all manner of books came to be printed and widely circulated under King Edward's patronage.

After so many years of bloody warfare the peaceful relaxation of Edward's court came as a welcome relief to the sophisticates who had gathered themselves around their new king. It is true that King Edward led an abortive expeditionary force to and from France; a venture that proved as foolish and vainglorious as it was expensive. Some of the blame for Edward's defeat in France was attributed to the disloyalty of his brother George, Duke of Clarence, and it came as no great surprise when George was found dead under mysterious circumstances, drowned in a barrel of Malmsey wine. In age George was midway between King Edward and Richard, Duke of Gloucester, and the fact that George's death put Richard one step closer to the throne did not pass unnoticed. The loss of his brother did nothing to lessen Edward the Fourth's delight in being king. He lusted successfully after several women, an activity together with undisciplined eating and drinking which did not suggest either a long or a healthy life. Nevertheless his death at the age of forty-one on 9th April 1483 was both unexpected and unwelcome.

King Edward's demise should not have created a problem of succession, his two sons being young but healthy. Edward, the eldest, was twelve and immediately assumed the title of Edward the Fifth, his nine year old brother Richard having already been created Duke of York, although collectively the two boys are known to history as The Princes in the Tower. It is their fate which provides us with one of the most enduring of mystery stories.

Richard, Duke of Gloucester, had been as valiant, as loyal, and as trustworthy as any brother could be. It was therefore natural that Edward the Fourth's dying wish was to grant Richard the legal status of England's Lord Protector, whilst at the same time entrusting his sons into their uncle's care. King Edward's trust was not shared by his widow, Queen Elizabeth Woodville. The Queen had good reason for holding Richard in low esteem. For years there had been rumours that his was the hand that had murdered Henry the Sixth, that he had slain Prince Edward not *during* the Battle of Tewksbury but *after*, in cold blood. He had certainly been insensitive enough to marry Prince Edward's widow, Anne, herself the daughter of Warwick the Kingmaker. She in turn had died in mysterious circumstances. Some said that Richard had poisoned her in order to pave the way for a second marriage, this time to his neice Elizabeth, daughter of Edward the Fourth; a marriage so objectionable it never took place. It was also widely believed that it was Richard who murdered his own brother George, Duke of Clarence, by drowning him in wine. Does all this indicate that Richard, Duke of Gloucester, was vile enough to kill his young nephews, the Princes in the Tower?

Shakespeare certainly thought so. He depicted Richard as having both a withered arm and a hunchback, a deformed baseless character capable of anything. Unfortunately, Shakespeare was writing his brilliant play *Richard the Third* a century later, and his only source of reference was *The Chronicles* written by Holinshed and published in 1587 when the Tudors were in control and unafraid of manipulating history to tarnish King Richard's reputation. Even so, leaving aside Shakespeare and Holinshed's biased account, there is enough evidence to suggest that Richard had both motive and opportunity to rid himself of the two boys who stood between himself and the throne of England.

Queen Elizabeth Woodville's first move was to seek sanctuary in Westminster Abbey with her youngest son Richard, Duke of York; Edward the boy-king already enjoyed the doubtful protection of his Uncle Richard. Under threat of physical violence the Queen allowed young Richard to join his brother in the Tower of London, ostensibly so that both boys could be prepared for the forthcoming coronation. Neither boy was ever seen again. The one man of honour and principle who might have been able to protect them, Lord Hastings, was executed without trial by the orders of Richard on the flimsiest of pretexts.

A man with less honour and few principles was the Duke of Buckingham. He possessed a huge private army and was happy to ally himself with Richard simply because he loathed and hated the entire Woodville family. It was Buckingham who now produced evidence that when Edward the Fourth married Elizabeth Woodville he was already betrothed to a daughter of the Earl of Shrewsbury and that according to custom such a promise of marriage was equivalent to marriage itself. Therefore Edward's marriage to Elizabeth was invalid and their two sons were illegitimate and no longer in the line of succession.

With theatrical reluctance Richard allowed himself to be put forward as the next in line, tacitly ignoring the claims of Edward, young son of the drowned Duke of Clarence. Parliament and the King's Council were as confused as the kingdom at large, agreeing that Richard could now be crowned king. With a haste that was almost indecent King Richard the Third had his coronation almost at once, on 6th July 1483. The Princes in the Tower had now become irrelevant and there were stories that the boys were dead before Richard was crowned, although most evidence suggests they were killed a few weeks later.

In all probability the deed itself was carried out by two men of decidedly ill-repute, John Dighton and Miles Forrest. Equally certain is the fact that these ruffians were hired by Sir James Tyrell, who later hanged for the crime; although his execution did not take place until nineteen years after the crime, in 1502, and even then his so-called confession was never made public nor did he have benefit of a recognised trial. The mystery still remains of how Tyrell gained access to the boys. At this time the Constable of the Tower of London was Sir Robert Brackenbury, a close friend of Richard's and responsible for the protection of everyone within the Tower, so for this reason alone he must have been party to any conspiracy. Of the quartet of Dighton, Forrest, Tyrell and Brackenbury only Tyrell was accused of the crime, and by that time King Richard was dead.

The Duke of Buckingham may well have had reasons of his own for seeing the sons of Queen Elizabeth Woodville dead, but, as if to complicate matters further, he chose the period immediately following King Richard's coronation to turn against him and try to defeat Richard by force, rather as a previous kingmaker, the Earl of Warwick had done, and with the same result. In a pitched battle to the south-west of London Buckingham was beaten, to be executed as a traitor in the market place of Salisbury.

Many other notables of the time were executed without trial, especially members of the Woodville family. Divisions, factions and rivalries began to erupt and it was clear that England was close to anarchy again. It no longer mattered whether the rumours and stories about King Richard were true or false; the all-too-frequent blood-letting had created a situation that had become intolerable and unacceptable. Neither the Yorkists nor Woodvilles seemed able to live with each other and England had need of a knight in shining armour who would descend from the clouds and take control. The nearest to this paragon was Henry Tudor, the Earl of Richmond, who was preparing to abandon his self-imposed exile in France and land in Wales to gather support before marching to meet King Richard.

Henry Tudor's claim to the throne was extremely slender, based on a distant ancestry with John of Gaunt, Duke of Lancaster, son of Edward the Third. Henrys the Fourth, Fifth and Sixth had been descended from John of Gaunt's first wife, Blanche. By his third wife, Katherine Swynford, descent passed through his son and grandson to Lady Margaret Beaufort who married Edmund Tudor, son of Owen Tudor and Henry the Fifth's widow, Katherine de Valois. Lady Margaret's son, born when she was only thirteen years old, was Henry Tudor who, in 1485, was twenty-eight years old, intelligent, of a tall strong physique with hair already beginning to thin. His convoluted claim to be king owed everything to the earlier prompting of the Duke of Buckingham, who had urged him to use his indirect line of royal inheritance as justification to overthrow Richard the Third, a king whose unpopularity was growing day by day.

Henry Tudor was shrewd enough to take full advantage of his Welsh ancestry going back several generations, and he gathered support as he marched across Wales to confront King Richard.

Compared with other conflicts in the Wars of the Roses this coming battle was destined to be small-scale in numbers and time. The place was called Bosworth, almost in the centre of England, the date was 22nd August 1485, and in less than two hours it was all over.

To the north-east was King Richard with an army totalling about 10,000, many of whom were not anxious to fight, having little faith in their cause. Facing him to the south-west was Henry Tudor, with only 6,000 men, all of them anxious to please their new champion. Waiting in the wings, to one side, was Lord Stanley with his private army numbering 5,000; pledged to fight for Richard *and* for Henry. Lord Stanley's failure to support Richard immediately disheartened the king's men and in the heat of battle several sections of his army either defected to Henry Tudor or joined Lord Stanley to await developments. The issue was not long in doubt.

King Richard fought bravely; he always did; his personal courage was seldom in question. He was killed charging headlong towards the enemy, his golden crown firmly thrust onto his battle-helmet until he was unhorsed and the symbol of English kingship rolled under a bush; there it was retrieved by Lord Stanley and placed triumphantly on Henry's head.

With Richard dead, his body stripped and humped over a horse's back ready for an unceremonial burial, the line of Plantagenet kings stretching back to 1154 and Henry the Second was at an end. King Richard was thirty-three years old and he had reigned for only two years and two months. England stood at the threshold of a future which for the next 118 years would be dominated by five Tudor monarchs.

Henry the Seventh, victor at Bosworth, would be the first.

6

THE ENGLISH REFORMATION (1485 to 1553)

King Henry the Seventh would be unlikely to gain very high marks in any popularity contest between English kings. For one thing he gained the crown by conquest, a most un-English thing to do. For another he is chiefly remembered now as one of the most efficient tax-gatherers of all time, and such people are never popular. But perhaps our lack of enthusiasm for Henry Tudor is because of his great intelligence, and the English are well-known for distrusting monarchs who are too clever.

He revealed his intellects from the very beginning. Almost unknown to the general population, with an unconvincing claim to be their ruler, he nevertheless arrived in London direct from the battlefield at Bosworth with an air of supreme confidence, looking every inch like a King of England. It was an illusionist's trick in the grandest of grand manners and it worked. He was astute enough not to seek Parliament's consent for his coronation, merely their confirmation afterwards that his actions were lawful; no doubt they were too spellbound to disagree.

At no time did he proclaim his own ancestry to justify seizing the crown from Richard the Third; he reasoned that everyone was sick of war, that too many noble and influential families had either slain each other to extinction or were too dispirited to challenge the assumptions of their new king. For the people of England, 1485 and Bosworth must have seemed merely one incident in a never-ending struggle to find political stability and they imagined that Henry Tudor would, in time, be overthrown as easily as he had deposed King Richard.

King Henry's brilliance was evident again when he chose to marry Elizabeth of York, the daughter of Edward the Fourth. The union was popular and seemed to close the breach between Yorkists and Lancastrians; the white rose and red rose were now superimposed together to form the Tudor Rose; a symbol of unity which Henry adopted as his emblem. He remained unsure of his position as king throughout his reign although he was never seriously challenged by any of the individuals who could have claimed hereditary precedence over him. The two main attempts to disprove his rights were both by imposters, neither came remotely close to success, and either incident would today furnish a composer with an improbable plot for an inventive comic-opera.

The first attempt was made by Lambert Simnel, a boy of twelve claiming to be Edward, son of George, Duke of Clarence—the same duke drowned in a barrel of wine. Bearing in mind that the real Edward was imprisoned in the Tower of London, and could be produced on request, the claim was both preposterous and doomed to failure. Lambert Simnel was the son of an Oxford craftsman but his resemblence to Edward encouraged a group of Yorkists to smuggle the boy to Ireland, gather support and invade England. On 16th June 1487, near the village of Stoke, on the Rover Trent 3 miles south of Newark, King Henry's army met Lambert Simnel's forces led by the Earl of Lincoln. A short battle, during which most of the rebels were either killed, drowned or captured, resulted in an easy victory for King Henry and death for the Earl of Lincoln. It has been said that this Battle of Stoke deserves to be remembered as the final War of the Roses instead of Bosworth. Evidence of King Henry's magnaminity is shown by the fact that the boy Lambert Simnel was captured and put to work in the king's kitchen, where he continued to be a servant in the royal household until he died at the age of sixty.

The second attempt was also made by a boy, Perkin Warbeck, who purported to be Richard, Duke of York—the younger son of Edward the Fourth—one of the two 'Princes in the Tower'. In 1490 Perkin Warbeck was sixteen years old and although French-born and living in Flanders, he shared many physical character-istics with Edward the Fourth. Only a handful of discontented Yorkists were left to exploit Perkin Warbeck's appearance and coach him in his play-acting role, but to their delight many continental kings accepted the youth at his face value and entertained him as they would a royal king. All this was designed to undermine and embarrass Henry the Seventh who used every diplomatic manoeuvre possible to force Perkin Warbeck into the open. For nine years Perkin Warbeck drifted from one country to another, treated like a king and growing in confidence until he overreached himself. To support a minor rebellion he hoped would sweep him onto the throne of England he landed in Cornwall and was captured. Again Henry was lenient, putting the young man into an easy-going light imprisonment, until he escaped and was then imprisoned in the Tower of London in a cell next to Edward, the boy impersonated by Lambert Simnel. The two young men plotted together and King Henry had no alternative but to execute them both; Perkin Warbeck was hanged and Edward beheaded.

Meanwhile Henry the Seventh was strengthening his hold on the kingdom. For nearly two hundred years coins of the realm carried the head of Edward the First; Henry Tudor replaced them with coins bearing his own likeness. For over three hundred years English kings had been addressed as 'Your Grace'; now the title was inflated to 'Your Majesty'.

He was the first English king to recruit a bodyguard, the Yeoman of the Guard who still escort and protect the sovereign on important state occasions. Henry was fair minded enough to reward those who supported him and yet shrewd enough to ensure the reward was not so great that it encouraged too much self-importance or pride. He made few real friends and whilst not entirely unapproachable he remained aloof and constantly aware of his own dignity.

His reputation as an administrator and tax-gatherer was not based on new ideas or innovations; he simply made the existing machinery of government more efficient, less wasteful, and ensured that all taxes, duties and customs were paid in full. By careful and relentless husbandry, combined with his support of merchants and traders, he almost trebled the nation's income and its economy became the envy of Europe. His Archbishop of Canterbury was also his Chancellor responsible for tax-collection; Cardinal Morton. Some of Morton's ruthless methods are cited by economists today who still quote the maxim of 'Morton's Fork'. If a man known to be wealthy is acting the part of a miser then he is clearly not spending his money and can afford to pay his dues; on the other hand, if he entertains lavishly then he obviously has the capability to settle his tax account.

When the great scholar, Desiderius Erasmus, chose to settle in England during 1499 he elevated the academic life of Oxford University to new heights. England was developing a climate of freedom in which continental painters and sculptors could express themselves without fear of political or religious persecution and their influence served to encourage native-born talent. The full flowering would come during the reigns of Henry the Eighth and Elizabeth the First but it was Henry Tudor's court which laid the foundations. He was swift to encourage all the new artistic ideas sweeping across Europe and only in the new invention of printing did he express caution, anxious that a tidal-wave of tracts and pamphlets critical of the catholic church should not flood England, and he instituted some crude censorship to prevent the wholesale circulation of such material.

As the fifteenth century closed England's geographical isolation, at the western limit of the old world, was about to end. Spain and Portugal, supported by an edict from the Pope, had taken advantage of Columbus's voyages of discovery to carve out their own spheres of influence in what we now call South and Central America. Henry the Seventh was all too well aware that England, an island with maritime ambitions, ought to be involved. He empowered John Cabot and his sons, born in Italy but now citizens of Bristol to sail under the English flag and discover what lay to the west and north-west of Britain; a direction that would not conflict with the interests of Spain or Portugal. Sometime during the summer of 1497, Cabot discovered a 'new found land' to be known ever afterwards as Newfoundland. England had staked her first claim on the western continent of North America and her position in the world had shifted to centre-stage.

King Henry was conservative in his law-making, content to secure justice for all his subjects and uphold the laws enacted by Parliament. His one legacy was to establish a special tribunal in 1487 to short-circuit delays in the ancient law courts if some national interest was concerned. This tribunal met at the king's palace at Westminster in a chamber decorated with stars and it became known as the Star Chamber. In later generations the methods of this tribunal were abused and the name acquired a sinister meaning it did not have during the days of Henry the Seventh.

Elizabeth of York bore Henry two sons and three daughters. Their eldest daughter, Margaret, was married at the age of eleven to King James IV of Scotland, whose granddaughter was destined to achieve fame as Mary Queen of Scots. Their eldest son, Prince Arthur, was also the subject of a diplomatically important marriage; to Catherine of Aragon, a Spanish princess. Bride and groom were only fifteen years old but within four months Arthur was dead and Catherine a widow. This union had been so important to both countries that a special dispensation was made by the Pope allowing Catherine to marry her brother-in-law, Henry, the second son of King Henry the Seventh. All religious and doctrinal logic suggested that such a wedding ought not to be possible, with or without Catherine's assertion that her young husband had failed to consummate the marriage. However the Pope agreed to a union that would have fateful consequences for England, Europe and ultimately the world.

When King Henry the Seventh died on 22nd April 1509 he bequeathed to his son, Henry the Eighth, a nation that was solvent, at peace with its neighbours and itself, but, although Henry Tudor had brought the gift of political and economic stability to his kingdom, his unspectacular methods of government must have seemed dull after the excitements of previous reigns.

Henry the Eighth was eighteen years of age when he became king; a superb athlete, who excelled at every sport then in fashion, especially tennis and hunting. A series of lavish banquets and expensive pageantry to celebrate his coronation and his marriage to Catherine of Aragon were evidence enough that he intended to squander with rich abandon everything his father had accrued by strict economies.

Although Henry enjoyed meeting ambassadors and involving himself with European affairs, the dull routine of day-to-day government bored him, and he was happy to delegate much of this to Cardinal Wolsey, one of the most ambitious and corrupt men ever to enter the twin-professions of church and politics. However, in 1520, diplomacy and the world of extravagent fashion coincided. What today would be called a 'summit meeting' took place in France between King Henry and Francis I, not in a palace but in an open field near the town of Guisnes. For almost three weeks the 'upper crust' of high society from England and France dined together in an elaborately tented-village in an outward display of such wealthy ostentation that the event is known as 'The Field of the Cloth of Gold'. The guests were numbered in their tens of thousands and their servants provided the most expensive outdoor picnic in world history, with each king and each noble family attempting to upstage the others in luxury and self-indulgence. King Henry was at this time clean-shaven but he now grew a beard to emulate the French king. All this social and diplomatic intercourse went for nothing when two years later the English and French were fighting an inconclusive and expensive war in that same Field of the Cloth of Gold.

The king was certainly a pleasure-seeking individual and enjoyed all manner of lavish entertainments, yet he was not entirely frivolous. He could speak latin and French with ease, he mastered the art of musical composition ('Greensleeves' is attributable to King Henry's own hand) and as a student of theology he wrote, in 1521, an entire book denouncing Martin Luther which so impressed the Pope that he granted Henry the title *Fidei Defensor* (Defender of the Faith) still used by our present sovereign, appearing on coins in an abbreviated form 'Fid Def' or F.D. For almost twenty years Henry the Eighth reigned as a king inviting little or no controversy, putting his own personal comfort and convenience first without bothering overmuch with what was happening within his kingdom. Then, sometime in 1529, sexual-passion and religious-dogma combined to shatter the social, political, and spiritual life of England. It was a revolution in all but name and we call it The Reformation.

Henry had been increasingly disappointed in Catherine of Aragon's failure to produce a son; she had borne a daughter, Princess Mary, and had several still-born infants and miscarriages, but the king was increasingly desperate for a son to succeed him. At this moment he met Anne Boleyn and became convinced that she would be capable of producing his longed-for son, or perhaps he merely used this as a pretext to disguise the sexual attraction he felt for Anne, who made it clear she must be the king's wife or nothing. Divorce was the solution, on the grounds that his marriage to Catherine, his sister-in-law, had been unlawful.

Cardinal Wolsey, who had worked his way through the king's household to become Chancellor, was deputed to arrange for Pope Clement VII to annul the original dispensation and declare King Henry's marriage to Catherine dissolved—a mere formality if the pope so wished. Under political pressure from other European rulers who were related to Catherine, the Pope did not so wish; Wolsey had failed and the Pope and the King of England were on a collision course.

In an earlier age, or with a king less wilful than Henry, the matter might have ended there. Other kings had defied the Pope or quarrelled with the church—Henry the Second and Becket, King John and Archbishop Langton are two examples—but eventually all had been forced to accept the authority of Rome. This time things were different.

First of all the Protestantism of Martin Luther was gaining ground in Scandinavia and Germany, and although England was not yet collectively prepared to embrace all the principles of Lutheranism the groundswell of anti-clerical feeling was loud enough to be heard. The Church in England—and there was only one Church, the universal Catholic Church owing allegiance directly to Rome—was becoming too rich, too powerful, and too corrupt. Cardinal Wolsey, representing all that was unpopular, holding offices in name only but from which taxes and dues poured into his coffers, had built a palace for himself more magnificent than anything possessed by his king; Hampton Court. Parliament had been meeting only infrequently but the corruption of Wolsey and the Church had to be challenged, and, for different reasons, Parliament and king began to push together against the same door. Parliament was anti-cleric because of the financial power of the Church; almost a third of the kingdom was owned by the Church and much of its revenue was going to

Rome. The King's views were identical, with the addition of wanting parliament's moral support to defy the Pope and the Church and so find a way of divorcing Catherine and free himself to marry Anne.

Wolsey was dismissed from his office of Chancellor in 1530, and banished to York from where he was summoned to return and face charges of high treason. He died of heart-failure before reaching London. His place was taken by Sir Thomas More, a personal friend of King Henry's and a well-respected scholar, whose influential book 'Utopia' had recently been published. Although not an ordained clergyman he was a devout Catholic with orthodox views and he could clearly see the conflicts of loyalty that were ahead. King Henry's differences with the Pope concerning the divorce and control of the church were heightened when the king declared himself to be Supreme Head of the Church in England; the country's spiritual, as well as earthly, ruler.

Parliament fully supported the king. They had no collective soul to be endangered, and opposition was limited to those who supported Catherine as being the innocent victim of a power-struggle that had sexual overtones, and those with a religious conscience, who refused to accept King Henry as their spiritual leader. John Fisher, Bishop of Rochester, represented the former, and Sir Thomas More the latter. Both were executed, during the summer of 1535.

Meanwhile, in 1532, King Henry made two significant appointments. Thomas Cranmer, a bishop well-known for disapproving of Henry's marriage twenty years earlier, was promoted to Archbishop of Canterbury with instructions to investigate the legality of the king's union with Catherine and pronounce a divorce if appropriate. Thomas Cromwell, a merchant and lawyer who had learned much from Wolsey, was appointed as Chancellor to use his legal talents for making the divorce easy. The matter was infinitely delicate because Queen Catherine was very popular throughout England and the rest of Europe, and King Henry was anxious that the divorce proceedings be handled with dignity and respect for Catherine's position. Thomas Cromwell and Archbishop Cranmer proved equal to Henry's trust and in 1534 the divorce was made absolute. The following year, Parliament formally enacted the law confirming King Henry the Eighth as Supreme Head of the Church in England—a constitutional position still held by our present sovereign.

Thomas Cromwell is still regarded as one of the most astute and capable political administrators of all time, and he certainly steered King Henry's ship of state through some very rough waters. He reduced, with drastic efficiency, the power and influence of the church, seizing much of its treasure and giving it to the king. This was done by first of all investigating the wealth and size of some thousand monasteries that dominated both town and country; then, having assessed their value, Cromwell abolished them. What came to be known as the Dissolution of the Monasteries was exactly that: the silver and gold plate was confiscated, the stone outbuildings pulled down and the Church centre-piece either utilised as a general place of worship (like Westminster Abbey), converted into a nobleman's exotic country house (like Woburn Abbey, home of the present-day Duke of Bedford) or left ruinous to provide good quality stone for local building uses. The first-class farming land owned by monks and nuns was sold off cheaply and the entire economy of England gained a massive injection of new capital from which everyone benefited.

It was not, unfortunately, all pure gain. With the monasteries went many hospitals, schools, hostels for travellers and almshouses for the poor, although in time the state or local benefactors replaced the losses. King Henry ensured none of the homeless monks suffered and many were paid a handsome pension for life; probably from the massive influx of treasure and sale of monastery land.

For the general population little had changed. The king had a new wife, Anne Boleyn, who never became popular. The whole of Europe threatened to unite and restore, by force if necessary, the Pope's authority but it never did. Doctrinally, the technology of church services remained the same, masses continued to be said and sung as before, the only difference was to delete references to the Pope—known now as 'the bishop of Rome'—and substitute King Henry. Nevertheless, with no great Papal authority to make liturgical judgements, many bishops and theological students began to propound opinions that were unorthodox. Many individuals who favoured sentiments too pro-Rome were executed side-by-side with those favouring anti-Roman or Lutheran Protestantism. The church became not merely disunited but confused and lacking direction. For the first time ever, in 1538, a Bible translated into English by William Coverdale, was ordered to be placed in every church, but a year later Archbishop Cranmer introduced a different Bible, translated by William Tyndale, and this became the official standard Bible.

As for Anne Boleyn, she was proving herself no more capable of producing a son than her predecessor, although like Catherine she gave Henry a daughter, the future Queen Elizabeth. So, Thomas Cromwell, demonstrating his usefulness to the king yet again, 'found' adulterous evidence against Anne and after only a thousand days, and nights, as Henry's wife she was tried for high treason and executed on 19th May 1536. Eleven days later Henry married Jane Seymour who died in 1537 giving birth to Henry's only legitimate son, Edward. Their marriage had been short but happy, and it was Jane who reconciled her husband with the two princesses, Mary and Elizabeth. Nevertheless, Mary remained firmly pro-Rome and deeply resented the hurt done to her mother Catherine, conscious that if the marriage of her mother and father was indeed unlawful then her position as illegitimate had become impossible. For Mary a deep loyalty to Rome was not only spiritually important but had political advantages on earth too.

Thomas Cromwell, that most able and efficient Chancellor, now made a mistake. He urged the grief-stricken king to marry Anne of Cleves, daughter of a German duke, who could speak little or no English and had strong Protestant views. Holbein's portrait of her, commissioned by the king, flattered Anne, and for both partners the marriage was a disaster and Cromwell paid for it with his head. The wedding was on 6th January 1540. On 6th July the marriage was amicably dissolved (Anne of Cleves being given a handsome annual pension and outliving Henry by ten years). On 28th July the king married Katherine Howard and on 29th July Cromwell was beheaded. King Henry had become almost light-headed with irresponsibility and with a son growing confidently into boyhood he could afford to be sexually frivolous with young brides. Less than eighteen months later Katherine Howard shared the same fate as Anne Boleyn and for the same crime (adultery when married to the king was as great a treason as could be imagined) and in February 1542 she was beheaded in the Tower of London.

Henry ended his days with a wife who was more of a mother to him than a sex-kitten. Catherine Parr nursed him and made his palaces into homes, both for him and his three children. The king remained headstrong and uncontrollable to the end; corpulent through self-indulgent eating habits, with ulcerated legs which modern medicine can now cure in days but which gave him constant pain and inconvenience, and various internal diseases, he was a sick and irritable man.

King Henry the Eighth died on 28th January 1547 and he is buried in St George's Chapel, Windsor Castle, sharing the same grave as his favourite wife, Jane Seymour.

Was Henry the sadistic monster of popular fiction, remember-ed for having six wives and executing two of them? The bare facts make unpleasant reading. He became king in April 1509 and within months had executed Sir Richard Empson and Edmund Dudley, two of his father's efficient tax-gatherers, who viewed unfavourably the new king's profligacy with 'their' hard-earned money. The charges and evidence were pure fantasy and as a start to the reign the incident would have done credit to the Borgias. Even more horrific was the execution of Margaret, the Countess of Salisbury, in 1541: she had the double misfortune to be the last female Plantagenet and therefore a possible threat to the Tudor throne, and also the mother of Cardinal Pole who in France was preaching against Henry. She was sixty-eight years old and executed in a particularly brutal and bloody manner. It has been said that King Henry rarely showed clemency or mercy to anyone who offended him, that it is estimated 50,000 so-called criminals or religious heretics were hung during his reign, and his treatment of friends who offended him lacked not only loyalty but the benefit of common justice. Nevertheless, the king remained popular throughout his entire reign, perhaps because he always found men like Wolsey and Cromwell to be responsible for unpopular acts and who would take the blame and pay for it with their lives.

Throughout his reign of thirty-eight years he fought an almost continuous running battle against Scotland, in spite of his sister's marriage to King James IV, who, in 1513, was killed fighting the English at Flodden Field together with ten thousand of his brave Scottish subjects. The wars with Scotland stopped abruptly when Henry died, and the English army and navy withdrew. In France, Henry fought several inconclusive wars, none of them having much affect on the balance of power, which continued to sway to and fro between the continental nations. King Henry can deservedly be called Father of the English Navy because the design of his ships and all-round efficiency of his sailors improved and began a tradition of sound seamanship which England has never lost.

But, without doubt, the measure of King Henry's reign was to engineer a break from Rome. He did this without invoking organised resistance from vested interests in this country, without England being invaded by a combined force from the catholic continent, and without the Pope actively pursuing his authority against England with dedication and determination. If Henry's critics claim he was lucky, his supporters will merely say his courage deserved good fortune. England was now completely free and independent in a way that no other continental power could be and the real test would be if that independence could be maintained in a hostile world.

The son of King Henry and Jane Seymour was only nine years old in 1547 when he was crowned Edward the Sixth. He was intelligent beyond his years, taking an interest in politics, religion and the ill-disguised intrigue that pervaded life within the court.

However, of these three it was religion which continued to dominate everyone's attention, although Edward's reign was mercifully free of persecution. With Archbishop Cranmer, that kind and gentlest of men, leading the way, Protestantism was not only tolerated but becoming the accepted religion of everyone within the royal circle. Cranmer produced the English Prayer Book which allowed church congregations to pray together in their native tongue, a book that is still admired for its clarity and purity of the English language; four hundred years later it remains the yardstick by which other prayer-books are judged. Although it contained nothing to offend the old Catholic traditions there was no doubt, even then, that a real turning point had been reached. Hugh Latimer, one of England's leading theologians, joined Nicholas Ridley, the Bishop of London, in preaching openly of things that Henry the Eighth would have condemned as heresy. Religion was acquiring a human face, more relaxed and tolerant.

About this same time education became more freely available, not for every boy but for those whose fathers were craftsmen, small-time farmers and such-like. These were 'grammar schools', established in many towns under royal patronage, and their standard of teaching was exceptionally high, their pupils growing into manhood that twenty years later would enrich Elizabethan society. Wealthy noblemen continued for a time to provide individual tuition for their children, but it was soon evident that grammar schools gave a better all-round education and during the next hundred years private teaching ended in many households as the children of rich families became pupils of what were becoming known as 'public schools'.

The boy-king's first guardian and Lord Protector was Edward Seymour, Duke of Somerset (brother of Jane Seymour) although within two years he was deposed by John Dudley, Duke of Northumberland, who proceeded to mismanage the country into rampant inflation and near bankruptcy. Not surprisingly this made him generally unpopular and, looking ahead, he could see little future for himself and his Protestant friends if ever Princess Mary, an ultra-Catholic, should succeed as King Edward's natural heir.

Early in 1553, Northumberland's worst fears were realised when the king contracted consumption, a disease known to be incurable. The duke at once began to devise a scheme which would deprive Princess Mary of her birthright, seeking someone who was compliant, Protestant, and with a claim to England's throne which the people could accept. Unless Northumberland did this his own life would be forfeit and he used his influence to persuade the dying king to declare Lady Jane Grey his successor.

In July King Edward the sixth died, just before his sixteenth birthday, and once more England was plunged into a crisis of succession which this time would be intensified by a religious persecution of a kind not seen before in England.

7

MARY AND ELIZABETH

King Edward the Sixth died on 6th July 1553 but for two days news of his death was suppressed. This was to give the Duke of Northumberland an opportunity to place Lady Jane Grey firmly on the throne of England and seize Princess Mary before she could rally support for her cause. The duke failed to achieve either of his intentions and the opportunity never came again.

A few weeks earlier the young king had enthusiastically signed a document denying his Catholic half-sister Mary her natural birthright, bequeathing his crown instead to his Protestant cousin, Lady Jane Grey. This document had been endorsed by the king's council of ministers, only one man—Sir James Hales—refusing to sign, on the constitutional grounds that in 1544 Parliament had formally declared Princess Mary, Princess Elizabeth and then Lady Jane Grey *in that order*, should succeed Edward, and that no king of England had authority to override Parliament. Nevertheless, Lady Jane Grey was proclaimed queen and escorted in full state to her royal apartments in the Tower of London to prepare for her coronation.

The episode was a shameless attempt by Northumberland, England's Lord Protector, to retain power for himself: Lady Jane Grey was only fifteen years old, a great grand-daughter of Henry the Seventh, intelligent and attractive, but most important of all she had been married against her better judgement to the duke's youngest son, Lord Guildford Dudley. Northumberland's scheme was so transparent that the population would not accept it.

Meanwhile Princess Mary had evaded capture by Northumberland's men and was poised to flee the country, until it appeared obvious to her that she had overwhelming support from the people and this support grew stronger when she left Framlingham Castle, in Suffolk, and rode to London where she was welcomed with an enthusiasm and warm approval accorded to very few monarchs before or since. How much of Mary's popularity was due to her own personality and background and how much to dislike of Northumberland may never be known. Whatever the reason, Lady Jane Grey was now isolated and without support, obliged to remain in the Tower of London, not in pomp and state but under arrest, together with her unfortunate husband. She had reigned as queen for only nine days and it is debatable whether modern historians should dignify her with the title of Queen Jane, or merely refer to her as Lady Jane Grey. Some people believe her short reign was the origin of the phrase 'a nine day wonder'.

Queen Mary, on the other hand, was now in full control. A mature woman of thirty-seven who, with great courage, had held her Catholic faith and personal allegiance to Rome staunch and true during the difficult final years of her father's reign and throughout the surge of Protestantism when her half-brother Edward was king. At first she was merciful to those who had opposed her; only the Duke of Northumberland and two of his henchmen were executed for their high treason. Lady Jane Grey and her husband, together with Archbishop Cranmer, were also convicted of treason but they were neither pardoned nor released, nor were their death warrants signed; an early indication of how indecisive Mary could be. Only in pursuance of restoring Catholicism was she relentlessly stubborn and single-minded, almost at once swinging the country back to the old Catholic faith. An immediate problem was that many clergymen, married as the new Protestant faith allowed, had to return to celibacy, and several bishops were among those forced either to desert their wives or be dismissed from office. She also moved to suppress Cranmer's Book of Common Prayer and to restore masses in Latin, together with other incidentals of Catholic worship. Further early problems were those of seeking a foreign alliance to counter the ever-present threat from France, also finding a successor who would carry forward the bright torch of Catholicism. Mary was urged to solve both problems with one solution: marriage to Philip of Spain, a fierce Catholic who would father an appropriate heir and who would welcome England as an ally.

Mary herself was distinctly unenthusiastic. The very idea of sexual relations was repugnant to her and she questioned the barrier of age; Mary was thirty-seven and Philip twenty-six. Again she was indecisive, aware that such a marriage would not be popular in England.

As news of the proposed union with Spain became public knowledge some opposition to Mary surfaced, the most serious rebellion originating, as so many revolts had before, in Kent. This one was led by Sir Thomas Wyatt who was intent on preventing Queen Mary marrying a Spanish prince known to have violently anti-Protestant views. The rebellious army grew in numbers as it approached London until almost 7,000 determined and well-armed men were behind Wyatt, only to be defeated when they became trapped in the city's narrow streets. Although the rebellion was unsuccessful it made Mary feel insecure. Within a month she executed Lady Jane Grey and her husband, and for a time she imprisoned her half-sister Elizabeth on suspicion of complicity in Wyatt's rebellion; this was the occasion when Princess Elizabeth arrived at the Tower of London in pouring rain, desperately asserting her innocence and ever mindful that her mother, Anne Boleyn, had taken the same route through this entrance, now known as Traitor's Gate. No evidence was ever brought against Elizabeth and after two months she was released.

Mary, to give herself security and out of a sense of duty, married Philip of Spain at Winchester, in July 1554, and it cannot be a coincidence that so much persecution of unrepentant Protestants began after this date. In Spain the burning to death of heretics had become commonplace, but in England the spectacle was repellant, even among the most faithful of Catholics and both Mary and Philip became increasingly unpopular.

Among the first to endure the slow torture of being burned alive were the Protestant bishops, Hugh Latimer and Nicholas Ridley. As the flames consumed them, on 16th October 1554 in the Centre of Oxford, Ridley was heard to declare words that ring out as bravely now as they did then: 'We shall this day light such a candle by God's grace in England, as shall never be put out'. Archbishop Cranmer himself was soon to follow them into the fire as were almost 300 other religious dissidents during a reign of only five years, a number to contrast with less than a hundred during the 113 years reign of all the other Tudors put together.

This terrible religious persecution at home was matched by disaster overseas. To support her husband's campaign against France Mary sent an army to fight the French, a venture so unsuccessful that the English were forced to retreat from mainland Europe and surrender their last outpost, Calais, to the triumphant French. Mary is believed to have said: 'When I am dead and opened, you shall find 'Calais' lying in my heart'.

Philip of Spain stayed in England with Mary no more than fourteen months, and for the last two years of her life Mary relied more and more on Cardinal Pole, son of the Countess of Salisbury so cruelly executed by Henry the Eighth, who was now the Pope's representative in England. Mary and her cardinal continued to sentence and burn Protestant heretics to the very end, convinced that in restoring England to a Catholic union with Rome she was fulfilling God's work and in burning Protestants she was purifying their immortal souls.

On 17th November 1558 Queen Mary died; childless, deserted by her husband, and mourned by very few of the thousands who had welcomed her so warmly five years earlier. Those same thousands were now ready to cheer Mary's successor, her half-sister Elizabeth, daughter of Anne Boleyn and Henry the Eighth.

Queen Elizabeth the First was twenty-five years old at her coronation, blessed with many fine qualities and virtues, all of which she used to serve her country. Elizabeth loved England and the English people with a tireless devotion that rose above mere patriotism. She may be known as 'the virgin queen' but there is little doubt that she was married to her kingdom and it is not too fanciful to speak of her relationship with England in the same terms to describe a passionate love-affair.

She also had a gift for surrounding herself with wise advisers and of distinguishing between the advice of those who shared her love for England and those who sought advantage only for themselves. Someone who shared her patriotic love was Sir William Cecil, later to become Lord Burghley. As a Protestant he had served Edward the Sixth, but he discreetly embraced Catholicism whilst in Mary's government, and he was elevated by Elizabeth to be her Secretary of State—roughly comparable to a modern-day Prime Minister. Cecil could neither be corrupted nor persuaded into agreeing to anything not in the best interests of his country or his sovereign. His long partnership with Queen Elizabeth was to prosper during the first forty years of her forty-five year reign. When she referred to him as her 'Spirit' she was doing no more than acknowledging the exceptional way he served his queen and his country. Cecil is arguably the greatest and wisest statesmen England has ever produced and his contribution to the 'Elizabethan Golden Age' cannot be overstated.

Elizabeth's most immediate problem was yet again that of religion. The Pope's control of England's churches, and their revenues, had been broken by Henry the Eighth, although the king's religious doctrine was in essence no different from that practiced in France or Spain. Edward the Sixth and his advisers were more radical, and fully embraced extreme Protestantism. Mary had reverted back to an orthodox Catholicism, burnt those who disagreed, and at the same time accepted papal authority. Elizabeth was determined to steer a more moderate course. Accepting Cecil's advice, she returned to a form of Protestant worship that was tolerant, yet less radical than that of Edward the Sixth.

She was crowned at Westminster Abbey in a Protestant service; the Catholic mass in Latin was abolished, being replaced by Cranmer's English Book of Common Prayer; bibles in English translation reappeared and the sovereign resumed as Head of the Church, breaking Rome's power once again. Bishop John Foxe had compiled a massive book itemising in great detail religious persecution through the ages, adding a lengthy account of Mary Tudor's burnings. As a warning against intolerance Elizabeth ordered a copy of the book, known to us as Foxe's *Book of Martyrs* to be placed in every church and carried in every ship.

In truth, as seen through twentieth-century eyes, the differences between sixteenth-century Catholicism and Protestantism were small and centred upon the Protestant assertion that Communion bread and wine did not assume the properties of Christ's body and blood, and that to deny such transubstantiation was not heresy. In supporting this view Elizabeth risked a Catholic uprising in England, and invasion from France, bearing in mind the added complication of that country's special relationship with Scotland.

Since 1542 Mary Queen of Scots had reigned over Scotland. She was the granddaughter of Margaret, Henry the Eighth's sister, who had married James IV of Scotland, and so had a fair claim to the throne of England, with the added advantage for some people of being a staunch Catholic. By marrying the future King of France she was in a position to be a real threat to Elizabeth, especially when French troops were occupying Edinburgh and parts of Scotland close to the English border.

Early in 1560 the Scottish Protestants rebelled against the French Catholic occupation, and this gave Queen Elizabeth and Sir William Cecil their excuse to act. Sending every available soldier and naval ship to Scotland, the English forces defeated the French and enabled the Scottish Protestants to form what became a state-within-a-state; an enclave of Protestants with the rabble-rousing preacher John Knox to sustain them. With Mary Queen of Scots, her interfering mother, and Queen Elizabeth in mind, he complained loud and long at rule by 'this monstrous regiment of women'.

Spain, a strongly Catholic, pro-Rome country, might have been expected to intervene but Philip of Spain was entertaining an ambition to marry Elizabeth and thus renew his country's alliance with England.

Philip was not the only man with hopes of marrying Elizabeth. A feature of the early years of her reign was the way in which she kept potential overseas foes at bay by the simple expedient of remaining unmarried and suggesting she might marry first one foreign prince then another. It was a diplomatic juggling act which Elizabeth maintained for several years and it gained valuable time in which to build England's political and military strength.

She used similar tactics within her court, enjoying the sight of attractive and intelligent men rivalling each other to be her especial favourite of the moment—men such as Christopher Hatton, a lawyer in his early twenties who taught the queen to dance, and who rose to become Lord Chancellor. Another was Robert Dudley, son of the unpopular Duke of Northumberland executed by Queen Mary, he was created Earl of Leicester and became very special to Elizabeth over a long period of time; she called him 'Sweet Robin'. It was rumoured that Leicester murdered his wife Amy Robesart so that he could be free to marry the queen, but she would have none of this. Robert Devereux, Earl of Essex, was yet another with ambitions to marry Elizabeth and towards the end of her reign he was becoming so arrogant and ambitious that he turned against Queen Elizabeth and was executed for high treason, an event the queen regretted after signing his death warrant. Sir Walter Raleigh was another good looking and ambitious man who might have had hopes of marrying his queen. There seems a strong probability of truth in the story of how he laid his cloak on a muddy path to let Elizabeth keep her feet dry. Only when he married one of the queen's Ladies in Waiting did he lose favour and find himself imprisoned in the Tower of London. What is most remarkable about Queen Elizabeth's many flirtations, and about the way she liked to be flattered by handsome young men, is that she would not allow them to interfere in affairs of state; she seldom allowed her heart to rule her head.

Queen Elizabeth totally enjoyed the experience of being queen, of being surrounded by men rich in intellect who deferred to her; she listened, she respected their judgements, but she made the decisions. She paraded herself through her kingdom in a series of 'Progresses', passing from town to town, allowing her subjects to see her wearing fine clothes and expensive jewellery as she passed by in a coach or open litter. Such a display might, in some countries, have led to rebellion or revolution inspired by envy, but in England the people applauded Elizabeth wherever she went, even in the north where Catholicism was stronger than in the south.

During these Royal Progresses she was treated to lavish hospitality by members of the land-owning aristocracy so that the queen actually saved on her own household expenses by travelling. The very fact that Elizabeth showed herself to her people at a time when travelling long distances was uncomfortable cemented the bond between sovereign and subject and made Elizabeth's love-affair with her kingdom into a two-way process. By 1587 queen and country were on the edge of a crisis that would test their unity and mutual love.

Because of her ancestry, Mary Queen of Scots was accepted as being the heir to England's throne, always assuming Elizabeth did not marry and produce children. Mary was a Catholic at a time when Scotland was turning towards an extreme form of Protestantism, similar to that which had already swept over Scandinavia. When her husband, the King of France, died, she married an Englishman of royal blood, Henry Stuart, Lord Darnley, their son being destined to become King James VI of Scotland, and to succeed Elizabeth as King James the First of England. In a succession of scandals an Italian, David Rizzio, who was on intimate terms with Mary Queen of Scots, was murdered in her presence, and soon afterwards Lord Darnley himself was assassinated. For her third husband Mary wed the Earl of Bothwell, a marriage that outraged the Scottish Protestant lords. They united to put the infant James on Scotland's throne, after first deposing Mary and placing her in prison. This sequence of events alarmed Queen Elizabeth who regarded 'kingship'—even of her enemies—as sacred, and rebellions as events to be crushed without mercy. Mary Queen of Scots today, Queen Elizabeth tomorrow.

Accordingly, Elizabeth secured the release of her cousin Mary and allowed her to cross the border into England where, for nineteen years from 1568 to 1587, she was held in a number of castles and secure country-houses. Contrary to popular fiction, Mary Queen of Scots was never held in the Tower of London, nor did she ever meet Elizabeth. To allow Mary free passage to France was too dangerous; from there she might encourage the Catholic French to invade England. To return her to Scotland and the rough justice of her many enemies would be unthinkable. To permit Mary total freedom within England was a possibility, in time, if she did not use her position as a leading Catholic to undermine Elizabeth's Protestant rule. Mary Queen of Scots did have supporters within English society, especially in the Catholic north and it was here, in 1571, where the Duke of Norfolk led a rebellion which needed all Elizabeth's strength and courage to defeat. Just so long as Mary lived on English soil, a focal point for Catholic dissidents, she was considered by Elizabeth as a threat, especially as England was totally alone in the world with no alliances to buttress her Protestant isolation.

Meanwhile the first tentative attempts to build on Cabot's journies across the Atlantic were beginning to bear fruit. Queen Elizabeth invested money in voyages of exploration by Sir Humphrey Gilbert, Sir John Hawkins and Sir Richard Grenville, who founded an early settlement in what is now called Florida. Sir Walter Raleigh brought tobacco and potatoes to this country after starting a colony on the eastern American seaboard, naming it, after England's virgin queen, Virginia. Sir Francis Drake created history by sailing round the world in the *Golden Hind*, fighting any Spanish ships he found in and around California as he sailed up America's Pacific coast. In truth, few of these early landings in America became permanent settlements, but what they did was create an appetite for starting colonies overseas and exploiting any new territory not already occupied by Europeans.

Even more important and dangerous was the increasing regularity with which English ships attacked Spanish galleons loaded with gold and silver from South America *en route* to Spain. The English ships were neither pirates nor part of the Royal Navy; they were called 'Privateers', privately owned by English merchants but having the queen's unofficial approval. At one and the same time she gratefully accepted a proportion of the booty, and to appease Spain she publicly repudiated her sailors' exploits. It was a game Elizabeth could not play indefinitely as Spain began to lose patience. Events now began to move swiftly.

During 1585 an army was sent to Holland to help the Dutch Protestants in their war against the Spanish Catholics who then occupied that part of Europe. Elizabeth was now firmly committed to assist any Protestants anywhere who fought against Catholic intolerance and Sir Francis Walsingham was instructed by Elizabeth to start a counter-espionage department and expose those Catholics suspected of undermining English Protestant society. This again focussed attention on Mary Queen of Scots and in 1587, after much agonised heart-searching, Elizabeth accepted her ministers' advice and ordered Mary to be executed; an event that sent shock-waves throughout the whole of Europe, but especially in Spain.

The execution, at Fotheringhay Castle, on 8th February 1587, almost coincided with Sir Francis Drake's impudence in sailing into Cadiz and destroying a Spanish armada then being assembled to invade England—Drake called it 'singeing the Spanish king's beard'. However, this only delayed the armada whilst new ships were built, and during the summer of 1588 Philip of Spain sent his great armada to invade England.

Elizabeth was very much aware of the dangers and she put all her trust and faith in the men who had already proved themselves in their small but highly mobile privateers, even though she knew they were outnumbered and outgunned by the Spanish galleons. Whether or not Sir Francis Drake insisted on finishing his game of bowls before sailing to attack the Spanish Armada is yet another story unsupported by firm evidence. Nevertheless, his confidence was matched by Elizabeth herself, who spoke these brave words to her army assembled at Tilbury: 'I have the body of a weak and feeble woman but the heart and stomach of a king, and a King of England too'.

Her proud defiance was rewarded when favourable winds carried English fire-ships among the Spanish galleons, burning some and causing the rest to scatter. A convenient gale sent the remaining Spaniards onto England's rocky shore or so disabled their rigging that their return to Spain was slow and inglorious. Drake, Hawkins and Frobisher had given Elizabeth a victory that proved decisive, even though England and Spain remained locked in war until both countries signed a peace treaty early the following century. Spain gained a victory of sorts when the Irish Catholics rebelled with even greater strength against Elizabeth's Protestantism, and the fighting on that unhappy island took on a new bitterness and a new purpose.

Ireland apart, from 1588 to 1603 the England of Elizabeth the First basked in a warm autumnal glow. Sir Thomas Gresham had already founded the Royal Exchange—a combination, in present-day terms, of stock exchange and department store—and Elizabeth's reign saw London replace Antwerp as Europe's centre of trade and commerce. Trade with the west was limited by the absence of established New World colonies, but to the east a steady stream of merchant adventurers were reaping a rich harvest. Furs from Russia, spices and silk from Africa and beyond, were now part of England's commercial life. A landmark was the foundation in 1599 of the East India Company, which began to secure trading links on the Indian sub-continent, and which in the next two hundred years would expand and secure for itself an independence that became, for England, both a benefit and a handicap.

When Cecil, now Lord Burghley, died in 1598, a whole new breed of ministers were in office, many of them impatient with their ageing queen's conservatism. Among them was Lord Burghley's son, Robert Cecil, who had assumed the mantle of Elizabeth's right-hand man. It was he who would form the administrative link between rule by a brilliant but fading queen, last of the Tudor dynasty, and the headstrong foolishness of James, son of Mary Queen of Scots, the first Stuart sovereign.

Queen Elizabeth's great achievement was in presiding over a long stable reign, relatively free of corruption and religious persecution. By defeating the Spanish Armada and resisting close alliances with any of the continental powers, including the Church of Rome, she had given England an opportunity to take advantage of her position as an island to pursue a method of parliamentary government that was unique and still experimental. She had also created a cultural atmosphere in which gifted men were free to express themselves.

So many men of talent and intellect made a contribution to what we now recognise as a golden age of self-expression that a complete list would prove tiresome. Composers like Morley, Byrd and Thomas Tallis wrote church music and madrigals that give as much pleasure now as in the sixteenth century; miniature portraits were elevated to a new art form by Nicholas Hilliard and Isaac Oliver; Edmund Spencer wrote splendid poetry, much of it in praise of Elizabeth; and in the theatre a new tradition of dramatic writing was beginning. Christopher Marlowe at last found an outlet for his wayward genius, so too did Ben Jonson; nevertheless, the real glory belongs to William Shakespeare. He was born in Stratford on Avon in 1564 and died there in 1616 so that his active working life was almost entirely Elizabethan.

Queen Elizabeth the First, Good Queen Bess, sometimes called Gloriana, died in Richmond Palace on 24th March 1603, at the age of sixty-nine, having steered England through much troubled water for almost forty-five years. Protestants in England and northern Europe have cause to be grateful to her and she offered safe refuge to those who fled in their thousands from religious persecution in France. Whole generations of historians and writers have created a virtual industry on the subject of Elizabeth, finding in her character a woman of great courage and political skill, a woman of tolerance and culture, but above all else a woman who loved her country more faithfully than she could any of her handsome admirers.

8

KING AGAINST PARLIAMENT (1603 to 1660)

During the sixteenth century Scotland was a poor impoverished country. The land had never been as fertile as England's and there was no lucrative wool-trade to sustain the faltering economy of a country that was, due to its geography, largely wild and untamed. King James VI had been its monarch since infancy, when his mother Mary Queen of Scots had been deposed, and now, in 1603 at the age of thirty-seven, as poor and impoverished as his native country, he succeeded Elizabeth the First as King James the First of England.

Riding four hundred miles south from Edinburgh to London, with a motley band of relatives and retainers, each one as penniless as the other, James could hardly fail to be impressed by the wealth and prosperity of what he saw. Even if England was not a land flowing with milk and honey—the continuing struggle with Spain and the drain of resources in Ireland were proving too expensive for that—the contrast with Scotland was still marked and impressive. Henry the Eighth's dissolution of the monasteries and consequent redistribution of church lands had created a strata of society mid-way between the traditional land-owning aristocracy, and the hard-working but poor peasant; this was 'the gentry'. Some were influential in towns as merchants or lawyers but most were owners of prosperous and moderately sized country estates. This 'gentry class' was becoming increasingly important, forming a majority membership of the House of Commons as a counter-weight to the bishops, law-lords, and hereditary noblemen who comprised the House of Lords.

At the lower end of the social scale serfs and peasants had long since gained their total freedom even though many were still dependant on wealthy land-owners for their livelihood. Domestic conditions were far from ideal and yet the labouring classes enjoyed a rustic contentment several degrees higher than that prevailing on the continent or in Scotland. Unfortunately for everyone, England's new king decided to ignore or misinterpret the differences between English and Scottish society.

King James arrived in London with the reputation of having ruled Scotland with a dexterity comparable with that of Queen Elizabeth. For over twenty years he had successfully kept the Scottish clans apart, knowing when to be firm and when to make concessions. To maintain traditional links with Scandinavia he had married Anne of Denmark, daughter of a Danish king, and she had produced seven children of which only three, Henry, Charles and Elizabeth, survived beyond childhood, and even Henry was to die before reaching manhood. In his younger days James was regarded as an intellectual, quick-witted and endowed with the sort of wisdom that impressed everyone who met him. Sadly, to this he added a reputation for vulgarity, obscenity, bad-manners and a lack of the social graces England now expected from their sovereigns. He was already vain and conceited and he foolishly imagined that the early enthusiasm and deference he received in England was due to the charisma of his own personality and not to his status as king.

He deluded himself that such wealth as England possessed belonged to him personally and that he could rule as an absolute monarch without the restraint of Parliament, an institution he never understood. The sole advantage he gave to England and Scotland was to unify the crowns of both countries without destroying their separate characteristics. A full and formal unification would not follow for a hundred years, and even then the system of law in Scotland would remain different in many important respects from that of England.

The transition from Elizabethan to Stuart rule was smooth, due almost entirely to Robert Cecil, who served as Secretary of State to Elizabeth in her final years and to James in his early years. For once religion was not an issue to divide the people, as it had before when power passed from one sovereign to another during the Tudor period.

James was the son of a Catholic queen, Mary Queen of Scots, but was nurtured into manhood by men who favoured an extreme form of Protestantism then peculiar to Scotland—Presbyters, who founded a church without bishops or any of the formal trappings associated with Catholicism. Their equivalent in England, the Puritans—whose aim was to 'purify' the church of popery and all imagery—held high hopes of James giving the English church a firm nudge in their direction. At the same time Catholics hoped that as the son of a pro-Catholic he would restore their religion to pre-eminence again. The king resolved the issue with tact by presiding over a religious conference at Hampton Court Palace in 1604.

The outcome disappointed Puritans and Catholics alike, with the 'High Church Protestantism' of Elizabethan England remaining virtually unchanged. The most important decision of that conference was to authorise a new English version of the bible and this was eventually published in 1611. Still known today as The Authorised Version, it remains the bible accepted in every English-speaking country and probably represents the English language at its very best; appearing in the age of Shakespeare and on the threshold of Milton, how could it be otherwise?

Also in 1604 King James engineered a peace treaty with Spain which dashed the hopes of English Catholics who dreamed of Spaniards invading England to restore, by force, the 'true religion'. A small group of religious fanatics now planned a drastic move to remove not only their king but Parliament too.

On 5th November 1605 King James was due to open Parliament—as our present sovereign does annually, and often on a date within a day or so of the ill-fated plot—and a group of conspirators, including Guy Fawkes, planted several kegs of gunpowder in the cellars of Parliament, intending to explode them when the king and Parliament were duly assembled in the room above. News of the plan reached official ears and the plotters were arrested, some on a hill to the north of London from where they hoped to witness the explosion; it is still called Parliament Hill Fields. November the Fifth continues to be celebrated with firework displays and the burning of Guy Fawkes in effigy. Guy Fawkes and his friends may have thought England not Catholic enough, on the other hand some Puritans thought the prevailing 'high-church-Protestantism' was still too close to ritual Catholicism. Known as the Pilgrim Fathers they sailed to a new life in North America aboard the *Mayflower* and started to colonise the fertile land off America's eastern seaboard.

Meanwhile king and Parliament co-existed in a modicum of harmony, with Robert Cecil—now the Earl of Salisbury—trying to prevent James spending too much money. When Salisbury died in 1612, disillusioned and despairing, his position was not immediately replaced and King James was at last free to indulge himself, bringing England close to ruin with a lavish generosity which was not merely a weakness but an expensive habit the country could not afford. He devoted himself to a life of self-indulgent pleasure, resenting any suggestion that he should travel within his kingdom and show himself as Queen Elizabeth had done. He bestowed honours and titles far and wide, selling the newly created hereditary knighthood, called a 'baronetcy' to raise money. James openly revealed himself as a homosexual although that, in itself was not a political or social disaster, being regarded as an 'Imperial Vice'; the pages of Classical History show many instances of this and it was therefore deemed acceptable. What was unacceptable was that the king introduced so many unsuitable young men into government and elevated them to positions of great power and influence.

Robert Carr, a young and personable Scotsman who had accompanied the king from Scotland was an early recipient of the king's bounty, rising from nowhere to be Earl of Somerset in little more than five years. His attempt to influence foreign and religious policy by urging the king's son, Charles, to marry into the Spanish royal family ended in a diplomatic fiasco, and when he was involved in a sexual scandal and suspected of poisoning a prisoner held in the Tower of London, he was faced with social oblivion from which even the king could not save him.

Into his shoes stepped another young man who was to have a decisive influence on English history; George Villiers, the son of a country knight and an ambitious mother who was astute enough to appreciate the value of her son's physical attractiveness and effeminate social graces.

King James fell in love with Villiers from the moment he appeared at court. The king doted on him and they exchanged letters that record in intimate detail a young man's dog-like devotion, and the king's senile baby-talk of love. Rising quickly up the aristocratic ladder George Villiers found himself the first non-royal duke to be created for almost one hundred years and as Duke of Buckingham, he and his family continued to be loaded with honours, titles and positions of power and responsibility. In 1619 he was created Lord Admiral of England and became embroiled in yet another plan to marry Prince Charles with a Spanish princess. Charles and Buckingham travelled secretly to Spain only to return humiliated and rebuffed.

The reason why Buckingham and Prince Charles risked the reputation of themselves and their country was this: Elizabeth, sister of Charles and daughter of King James, had married Frederick the Protestant King of Bohemia and that part of mid-Europe called the Rhineland-Palatine. The Spanish-Catholics had deprived them of their throne and Buckingham foolishly imagined that an Anglo-Spanish marriage would restore Elizabeth and Frederick at least to the Rhineland part of their kingdom. Elizabeth is now remembered as the 'Winter Queen' for her brief seasonal reign, and also because she was the grandmother of a future King of England, George the First.

Buckingham's ignoble failure led him to demand war with Spain which the king agreed to only with reluctance but which Parliament starved of money. So Buckingham embarked on a war with Spain that was doomed to fail, heaping still more humiliation and dishonour on himself, his king and Parliament.

King James was a true pacifist who loathed war. He allowed the navy, built by Henry the Eighth and strengthened by Elizabeth, to melt away and the army to stand down; a rusty sword in a threadbare scabbard. His eagerness to appease potential enemies is illustrated by his treatment of Sir Walter Raleigh, the soldier and coloniser of America who introduced both tobacco and potatoes to England. In prison for thirteen years accused of treason against King James, he was released to lead an expedition for gold in South America. When the Spaniards complained at Raleigh's incursions into their sphere of influence King James not only failed to support him but proceeded to execute him for the treason committed thirteen years earlier; the incident was neither honourable nor wise and the king became even less popular as a result. King Henry IV of France once described James as 'The wisest fool in Christendom' and that epithet remains a fair summing up of England's first Stuart monarch.

The king became increasingly frustrated at his inability to exercise power without the restraint of a Parliament he found irksome. He is on record as declaring: 'I am surprised that my ancestors should have permitted such an institution to come into existence'. His creed of ruling alone, sanctioned only by Almighty God, was enshrined in his theory of the Divine Right of Kings and when he died on Sunday 27th March 1625 his son, Charles, aided and abetted by Buckingham, continued to push his father's theory to its limit.

King Charles the First began his reign by marrying a strongly Catholic French princess, Henrietta Maria, and England's religion lurched a little closer to outright Catholicism. This prompted further migrations to North America following in *Mayflower's* pioneering wake. It was England's strength to allow such dissident Puritans to leave with goodwill, free to establish a new life on foreign soil but under the English flag and with a loyalty to their native land. To prefer a more relaxed religion did not mean the Puritans wanted to abandon the advantages of Magna Carta or the protection of a Common Law which was fair to everyone.

Although as arrogant, vain and aloof as his father, it is possible Charles might have come to terms with Parliament and with his critics if Buckingham had not continued as chief minister, and the king's favourite. There is no suggestion that their relationship was homosexual but Charles greatly admired the duke and together they pursued war against Spain and France. Parliament disapproved of the war—especially when it began to disrupt trade and allow the emerging Dutch merchants to take advantage—and disapproved even more of Buckingham's influence.

For many hundreds of years English kings and queens had learned to govern through Parliament, recognising that they could only enforce those laws enacted by both Houses of Parliament. Constitutionally, the king was free to decide foreign policy, wage war or sign peace treaties, appoint judges and select his own ministers and advisers. His ultimate weapon was to dismiss and open Parliament as and when he wished, but Parliament itself raised revenue and levied taxes and also decided where such monies were spent. They also formulated law as 'Acts of Parliament' to which the king was obliged to give his consent. When some judges made rulings unfavourable to King James and King Charles they were dismissed from office only to be elected to the House of Commons where their incisive legal minds troubled the king even more. Parliament, or rather the House of Commons, was not yet a unified instrument of opposition but that was the direction it was taking as King Charles forced land-owners to lend him money and billetted soldiers in private households to be housed and fed. As a compromise, the impoverished king had to accept a Bill of Rights which would further limit his powers in return for money.

At this point, in August 1628, the Duke of Buckingham was assassinated in Portsmouth and the entire country rejoiced. Peace with Spain and France followed almost immediately. Parliament took advantage of the incident to pass a resolution against popery and against moves by the king to raise money for himself by unconstitutional means. King Charles retaliated by disbanding Parliament for eleven years, deciding the Divine Right of Kings gave him the authority to rule autocratically.

There remained only one check on the king's assumption of total power and that was England's Common Law, but even this could be circumvented as the king held the prerogative of appointing and dismissing judges as and when he wished. A leading parliamentarian, Sir John Eliot, who merely incurred the king's displeasure, was committed to the Tower of London; Sir Edward Coke, however, avoided the same fate although he campaigned loud, long and successfully to maintain the legality of Common Law.

King Charles had the support of two clever men: William Laud who became Archbishop of Canterbury and directed the English Church to move closer to a form of worship that was almost, if not quite, Catholicism, stamping out non-conformist Puritans whenever and wherever he could. The second man was Thomas

Wentworth, created Earl of Strafford, who had served both James and Charles in Ireland using a brutality that alienated Catholics and Protestants alike. He was now given the responsibility of governing the north of England and using his talent for bullying to keep King Charles secure on his throne.

By nature a quiet man, Charles was a great art connoisseur who accumulated a vast collection of some 1,400 paintings and 350 items of sculpture. It was he who employed Rubens, Van Dyck and Inigo Jones. He recognised the quality of Titian and masters from every European school of art, beginning a tapestry factory at Mortlake near London with designs painted by one of the world's greatest painters, Raphael. Even though some of this collection was scattered and sold by Cromwell many paintings still remain in the royal collection and many more formed the nucleus of England's various public art galleries. Nevertheless, King Charles's patronage of the arts cannot disguise the fact that he seldom acted in his country's best interests.

Parliament was reconvened in April 1640 but when it showed itself to be as defiant as its predecessor it was immediately dissolved, becoming known as 'the short Parliament' and the next Parliament, opening later the same year, remained in session, on and off, until 1660 and, not surprisingly, is known as 'the long Parliament'.

The Scots had rebelled against the imposition of Laud's religious policy and Parliament was in sympathy with Scotland and out of sympathy with both Laud and Strafford's ruthless campaigning. Even so the king might have survived Parliament's opposition to his Scottish policy if another issue had not arisen to unify the House of Commons against him. John Hampden, a land-owning member of Parliament representing an inland area, decided not to pay a tax—called 'Ship Money'—which the king had a constitutional right to levy on coastal towns for the provision of warships and other defences. When Hampden was taken to a Court of Law the royalist judges declared the king had acted within the law by taxing inland areas. Parliament disagreed and leading the House of Commons in their arguments against the king was a forceful character called John Pym. He outmanoeuvred King Charles in every direction, even forcing him to assent to the execution of Strafford on 12th May 1641; Laud's execution was to follow four years later. The defiant stand taken by Hampden against the imposition of widespread taxation disguised as Ship Money came to a head on 4th January 1642 when the king descended on Parliament in person, intending to arrest five members, including Hampden and Pym.

Given warning, the five fled and the Speaker of the House of Commons—at that time regarded as the sovereign's representative—refused to indicate their whereabouts. Every attempt by King Charles to locate the five men was frustrated and opposition to the king was now in the open, although actual hostilities did not begin until the king raised his royal standard at Nottingham in August 1642.

England's Civil War was not a rebellion, an uprising of common people against oppression, nor was it always the Catholic or high-church faction against Puritans and free-thinkers, although that too was an element. Families became divided, as did every strata of society; fathers really did fight their sons, and brothers found themselves on opposing sides. It was impossible to draw a territorial map of land won or lost at any given stage of the conflict; but as a guide it can be said the south and east, including London and all the seaports trading with Europe, favoured the Parliamentarians (called Roundheads because so many wore their hair cut short), the west and north favoured the royalists (Cavaliers because it was the most pronouncable equivalent of *caballeros* who were Spanish and devout catholic). Some Scots supported the puritans, others gave their sympathy but not much practical help to the king.

On 23rd October 1642 the first battle took place at Edgehill, west of Oxford, a small skirmish claimed by both sides as a victory. It was noteworthy because Oliver Cromwell—a land-owning member of Parliament from Huntingdon, and a radical Puritan—arrived on the scene in command of the Roundhead's cavalry. Although he was forty-three years old and had no military experience, he became such a successful cavalry commander that his prestige rose with every battle he fought. He and Sir Thomas Fairfax—Parliament's army Commander in Chief—organised their forces into a highly disciplined Model Army of Puritans who felt God had entrusted them with a great mission. The royalist army was less well-organised and they too felt themselves to be possessed of a mission, even if only that of ensuring their king maintained his right to rule. Their hero became Prince Rupert of the Rhine (nephew of the king, son of Elizabeth of Bohemia) who fought with a flair and courage that inspired every section of his army.

After the opening of hostilities public opinion demanded that Parliament and king should try and settle their differences by negotiation. Neither Roundheads nor Cavaliers chose to be very serious about peace terms and the real shooting war began again in earnest.

Bows and arrows had long been obsolete and although heavy cannons, muskets and hand-held guns were the weapons most in evidence there was still a place for infantry using pikes and dependant on tough leather jerkins for protection. Nevertheless, it was the cavalry which was to prove decisive as Cromwell quickly learned how to use his mounted soldiers in one successful battle after another. At Marston Moor, west of York, on 2nd and 3rd July 1644 the royalists were given a defeat so severe that the war should have ended there and then. Prince Rupert bravely regrouped his forces and a year later, further south at Naseby, he was beaten again; the combination of Fairfax and Cromwell was too much for the Cavalier army growing desperately short of food and ammunition.

King Charles very seldom moved from his headquarters in Oxford but in 1646 he moved north to enlist help from the Scots. Unfortunately, his lack of diplomatic skill, and stubborn insistance on religious conditions went against him and somewhere near Newcastle the Scottish forces abandoned him and returned home. The king was captured and brought south under armed escort, having lost a war he never looked like winning and it was only the bravery and dashing persistance of Prince Rupert and his brother Maurice which extended the conflict so long. But, having won, Parliament had no idea to what use the victory should be put.

As he travelled south the king was saluted with enthusiasm even though he was a prisoner, and he began to display a royal dignity as if on a stately progress. He imagined having to concede a few points here and there, taking heart from Parliament's growning disunity. The Model Army had not been paid and had been infiltrated by 'Levellers'—radical revolutionaries who wanted to control Parliament and end the monarchy—and they had the weapons to turn on their own moderate officers if necessary. Once again the slogan heard on Blackheath in 1381 during the Peasants' Revolt was repeated: When Adam delved and Eve span, Who was then the gentleman?'

Charles had been held in Hampton Court Palace from where he escaped on 11th November 1647 only to surrender to Robert Hammond, parliamentary governor of the Isle of Wight. For a further year the king was imprisoned on the island, in Carisbrooke Castle, and like Mary Queen of Scots in similar circumstances he began to intrigue and plot not just his escape but the overthrow of Parliament with Scottish assistance.

A second full-scale Civil War to restore Charles on his throne began early in May 1648 with an uprising to support the king in many counties. The Scots swept south as far as Preston in Lancashire. Here they met Cromwell's forces and were defeated. The parliamentarians had won again, but what of the king?

Negotiations between Charles and Parliament came to nothing and almost inevitably the extreme radicals in the army lost patience: The House of Lords and the institution of monarchy were formally abolished as King Charles was obliged to stand trial for his life. He refused to recognise the court's authority and remained disdainful and contemptuous of the proceedings, behaving with a quiet reservation throughout his ordeal. Fifty-nine commissioners signed the king's death warrant—Oliver Cromwell's among them—and on a cold winter's morning, 30th January 1649, King Charles the First stepped onto the scaffold erected outside his own Banqueting House in Whitehall and was beheaded.

Stubborn, vain, and courageous he faced death calmly and bravely, content that he was being martyred and that his sons, Princes Charles and Prince James, were safe in France.

John Hampden had been killed in battle and John Pym had died of natural causes leaving Cromwell and his triumphant

Puritans to control Parliament, aware that a well-trained army would ensure their decisions would be paramount. John Milton was an ardent supporter of Cromwell and his writings do much to illuminate the revolutionary optimism of those idealistic days.

The army had forced all but the most radical members of Parliament away and for a time they savoured the fruits of victory. Theatres and places of entertainment were closed; so too were racecourses to deny the moderately-minded gentry an opportunity to meet and express their disapproval of what was happening. The parliamentary gentlemen had supported moves to curb the king's power, but not his execution nor the revolutionary anarchy into which England was rapidly sinking. Business confidence evaporated; merchants were unable to trade freely and farmers discovered their workers preferred the life of a revolutionary soldier to ploughing fields.

Only in foreign affairs did Cromwell claim success. With the aid of Robert Blake—one of England's very greatest admirals—he created a formidable navy and used it to defeat not only the Dutch but every navy which dared to challenge the country's naval supremacy. In Ireland, Cromwell ruthlessly crushed the dissident Catholics in a brutal measure which ensured his name is hated there even in the twentieth century.

In 1653 Cromwell was formally declared 'Lord Protector' in a ceremony during which he sat enthroned on the famous coronation chair; undoubtedly he would have been crowned king if the republican army had allowed him such an honour. For a further five years he struggled to control the over-zealous Puritans and so gain that popular support without which he could not govern. For centuries England had evolved a twin system of rule by a combination of Crown and Parliament; King Charles had come to grief by attempting to rule as an absolute monarch, and now the Puritans were finding their version of government without popular consent equally impossible. The gentry and moderately-minded citizens were excluded from Parliament, indeed anyone who could not match the refined purity of Cromwell found it difficult to retain authority or responsibility.

When Oliver Cromwell died on 3rd September 1658 his son Richard replaced him as Lord Protector. Lacking both the

appetite for power and political skill of his father he was in office
for only a brief period. More and more people began to voice
their demand for a king to unify England again. Across the
channel such a king was waiting, Prince Charles, the eldest son of
Charles the First.

Only one man had the moral courage to take the initiative and
begin a course of action that would end in a restoration of the
monarchy; George Monck. He had fought as a royalist against
Cromwell, had changed sides and was now Parliament's military
commander in Scotland. Feeling no personal loyalty towards the
army commanders now squabbling among themselves in London,
Monck led his forces south early in 1660 and with perfect timing
began by persuading Parliament to allow the moderately-minded
gentry to return, where they promptly invited Princes Charles to
become England's new king. Monck behaved honourably and,
like the patriot he was, in his country's best interests, negotiating
with great skill until king and people were reconciled. When
King Charles the Second arrived he was greeted with warmth,
enthusiasm, and widespread relief that England had a king once
more.

By a happy coincidence, King Charles entered London on his
thirtieth birthday; 29th May 1660. He began his new reign in the
manner he would continue, sharing his royal bed with a mistress;
on this occasion she was Barbara Palmer. The contrast between
puritanical Cromwell and free-loving Charles would become
increasingly evident as theatres reopened, tavern entertainment
grew bawdier and a cheerful high-spirited gaiety possessed the
general population. A whole new life-style had erupted with
zestful immorality; we call it The Restoration.

9

THE RESTORATION (1660 to 1714)

Ten years before restoring England to a monarchy the second Charles travelled to Scotland, and there raised an army which he led into England in an attempt to gain the throne for himself as successor to his executed father, Charles the First.

Almost inevitably Cromwell defeated the royalists yet again and after the Battle of Worcester in 1651 Prince Charles, just twenty-one years old, became a fugitive. For six years he lived by his wits in the company of rough soldiers, lowly peasants and young wenches he shamelessly seduced. On one occasion he hid in an oak tree as Cromwell's men searched the ground beneath him; this is why so many English pubs are called *Royal Oak* and why members of institutions that owe their origins to King Charles the Second—such as the Royal Hospital in Chelsea—wear oak leaves in their coats each 29th May, the anniversary of the king's restoration to the throne and his birthday.

To raise his Scottish army Charles had to lie, make promises he could not keep, and agree to any proposal which furthered his own cause. All this cynicism and living (and sleeping) with the lower classes gave him an attitude to life he never lost. Whilst in exile in France and Holland he lived with a girl, Lucie Walters, who died before he became king. Nevertheless, their illegitimate son—one of fourteen who could claim Charles as their father— was created Duke of Monmouth and in due course this young man would try to claim that his mother had legally married Prince Charles, which put him in direct line of succession to England's crown.

King Charles the Second was generous in giving aristocratic titles to his bastard children and he similarly rewarded the husbands of his mistresses. In this way he could offer respectability to his ladies of pleasure and at the same time appease their husbands with somewhat meaningless titles and honours. Barbara Palmer—who slept with the king on his return to London on 29th May 1660—became Countess of Castelmaine when her husband Roger Palmer was elevated to the peerage. Nell Gwynne, who attracted the king's attention when she sold him oranges outside London's Drury Lane theatre, remained unmarried and had no title, although her illegitimate son was created Duke of St Albans; King Charles's dying words 'Let not poor Nelly starve' is the stuff of romantic fiction but in this case the story is true.

The king's marriage to a Portugese princess, Catherine of Braganza, did not diminish his sexual liaisons with other women; indeed after the wedding, his opportunities increased when he surrounded Catherine with a whole posse of his mistresses and designated them Ladies in Waiting (a superior form of aristocratic servant for the queen). This bevy of attractive and licentious women were immortalised by the court painter, Sir Peter Lely, who painted their individual portraits in a collection known as the Windsor Beauties currently on display in Hampton Court Palace. Among them a rival to Lady Castelmaine, Nell Gwynne, and the queen herself, a particular favourite of the king, Frances Stewart—'La Belle Stewart'—and it is her likeness as Britannia carrying a shield and trident that has continued to adorn our coins ever since. Even so King Charles the Second took care not to allow his private indiscretions to impinge on his public life, although he made no secret of his personal conduct.

Few kings can have led such a public life as Charles the Second: his palace of Whitehall was open to everyone as a sort of royal peepshow. Some came merely to witness the king dining in public but hundreds came to be physically touched by him in the hope of being cured of disease. All would have been impressed by his height, over six feet tall, and his unmistakable appearance; dark swarthy skin and eyes that were almost black. He could be seen almost every night at the theatre or in taverns of ill-repute, a King of England revelling in the sheer enjoyment of life and creating the legend of a merry monarch who never lost his common touch.

Charles was careful not to allow his nocturnal pleasures to distract him from matters of state. By day he steeped himself in the duties of ruling his kingdom with the same enthusiasm he gave to pleasures of the flesh at night. For several years he benefited from the advice and experience of Edward Hyde— created Earl of Clarendon, at the same time as another loyal adviser, George Monck, was made Duke of Albermarle. Clarendon had remained with the king during his exile and now became Lord Chancellor, a position of influence which increased further when his daughter, Anne, married the king's younger brother James; who would himself become King James the Second in due course.

Charles and Clarendon together decided not to take action against all the Roundhead parliamentarians who had opposed the Cavalier royalists, successfully limiting their revenge to executing those commissioners who had committed regicide (murder of the king) by signing the death warrant of Charles the First. Those regicides who had since died, such as Oliver Cromwell, had their graves opened and their corpses symbolically hanged by their rotting necks. As a public spectacle it was shocking and disgusting yet satisfying enough to close the episode and prevent other acts of vengeance against the Roundheads.

The new Parliament resented the king's policy of toleration, especially when land and property seized from the cavaliers during the civil war was not restored to them. The king's tolerance also extended towards religion as he swiftly realised that one consequence of his father's defeat was that Parliament and not the king controlled the form religious worship would take. Parliament, under Clarendon's leadership, enforced the Elizabethan concept of high-church Protestantism and both Catholics and Puritan-Presbytarians alike were made to conform; in Scotland this was achieved only by much bloodshed and repression.

Within five years of the king's restoration three disasters appeared in successive years, like bleak omens of the future. In 1665 a plague revaged London as seriously as the Black Death had in an earlier age. 'Bring out your dead' became a familiar cry as handcarts were trundled through the streets, piled high with disfigured victims of the terrible pestilence. At one stage a thousand people a day were dying until, in the following year, 1666, like a purifying Act of God, London was cleansed by the Great Fire as it destroyed four-fifths of the city. The devastation gave Sir Christopher Wren an opportunity to reveal his architectural genius and rebuild not only St Paul's Cathedral but many other churches too.

The third disaster came in the next year, 1667, when the Dutch—who had been at war with England for several years— impudently sailed up the River Thames and attacked the English fleet in their home waters, towing away the best of our ships, The Royal Charles, as their main prize. England felt the humiliation deeply and a swift peace treaty was signed.

Clarendon, whose arrogance had made him unpopular, was removed from office and in his place Charles appointed five individual ministers whose intrigues and in-fighting gave a new word to the English language. The initial letters of their names— Clifford, Ashley, Buckingham, Arlington and Lauderdale—form c-a-b-a-l and their opposition to each other led indirectly to the beginning of what eventually became 'party politics'.

The focus of their opposition was religion and the question of who would succeed the childless king. Prince James, brother of Charles, was the natural and logical heir but he was suspected of Catholic leanings. The Test Act—denying high office to those failing to repudiate transubstantiation (the old argument concerning Communion bread and wine, the very root and heart of Catholic belief) forced James to admit his true faith and he resigned his position as Lord High Admiral of England when he exiled himself in Scotland. His pro-Catholic supporters came to be called 'Tories' (from the Irish toraidhe meaning an Irish Catholic outlaw) whilst his protestant opponents were called 'Whigs' (from Whiggamores, Scottish rebels who held presbytarian views). In later years the Tories would develop into the modern Conservative party and Whigs into Liberals; although the religious aspect of their origins was lost when both political groups embraced all sections of Christian belief.

The Whigs were in favour of recognising King Charles the Second's illegitimate son, the Duke of Monmouth, as successor and although the king genuinely loved Monmouth and rejoiced that the young man was so popular and widely admired he knew this would ultimately prove divisive and rejected by the people, just as Lady Jane Grey had been disowned a hundred years earlier.

In order to be free financially of an increasingly disunited Parliament, Charles 'sold' England's foreign policy to France for a handsome annual subsidy, knowing he had the prerogative to wage war and sign peace treaties without Parliament's consent. King Charles saw it as selling a personal asset to a country he favoured and not, as it might appear to us, as an unscrupulously devious act which illustrated to perfection the moral bankruptcy of a king who had elevated all lack of principle to an expedient philosophy. France was soon invoking the king's right to wage war as the two countries combined against Holland, although England's navy had deteriorated by incompetence to the point when France derived little benefit from money paid to King Charles. So great was the confusion created by the king's foreign policy that Parliament at one stage imagined they were supporting the Dutch (protestants) against the French Catholics, whilst King Charles was ready to declare himself a Catholic if and when France crushed Holland, notwithstanding that his own nephew was now ruler of Holland.

English society was now divided for and against the king's policy, although such policy was far from clear. Charles defused a dangerous situation by disbanding Parliament and riding out the anti-Catholic storm that rippled through the country. A certain Titus Oates tried to stir up trouble with imaginary plots and everyone seemed to take him seriously except King Charles, who possibly recognised in Titus Oates a liar as brazen and barefaced as himself.

Whilst Catholic plots to murder Charles surfaced everywhere the king relaxed into the autumn of his life with an interest in horse racing, especially in the town of Newmarket which became what it is now, the sport's national headquarters. He continued to patronise the arts as composers like Henry Purcell, writers of the stature of John Bunyan and John Dryden, and painters such as Sir Peter Lely and Godfrey Kneller gave English society men to be admired worldwide.

Nevertheless, King Charles the Second will be best remembered for his formation of The Royal Society, a gathering together of
scientists, physicists and astronomers—men who were destined to
shape the future. Men like Sir Isaac Newton, Robert Boyle (called
the father of chemistry), Robert Hooke (inventor of balance
springs for watches), Sir Christopher Wren, Samuel Pepys (Secretary to the Admiralty, remembered by posterity for his diaries
which recorded the period so accurately) and John Evelyn
(another ship-building expert, whose excellent diaries have been
overshadowed by those of Pepys). This was the age when science
was born, when the Royal Observatory at Greenwich became
established and when enquiring minds started to question many
of the universal precepts which had been unchallenged for
centuries.

On 5th February 1685 King Charles the Second died, having
restored England to the rule of a monarchy. A man criticised for
his lack of principle but probably a man who had seen too much
of life to take it seriously; apologising for lingering on his
deathbed he was heard to say 'I am sorry gentlemen, for being
such an unconscionable time a-dying'.

In spite of the anti-Catholic voices raised against him, James
became England's next king; King James the Second. It was a short
reign that began badly and deteriorated sharply. He was not
intelligent and lacked the skill of his brother in keeping himself
free of controversy and accusations of bigotry. His first wife, Anne
Hyde—who had produced two daughters, Mary and Anne, both
destined to become Queens of England—had died in 1671 and
two years later he had married Mary of Modena, an Italian
princess who was so strongly Catholic that she was thought to be
a daughter of the Pope.

The succession of James as king split the country wide open
when he tried to impose his Catholicism upon English society.
Within six months the Duke of Monmouth brought an army of
supporters from Holland and arrived in the county of Somerset,
some two hundred miles south-west of London. Here he gained
more Protestant supporters who accepted his claim to be Charles
the Second's lawful son and heir. One battle was enough to crush
Monmouth's ineffective rebellion: it took place in early July, 1685,

at Sedgemoor and although Monmouth gained the initiative by attacking at night he was beaten without too much trouble. One of King James's military commanders at Sedgemoor was John Churchill, whose desertion of James three years later would change the face of England.

King James grew over-confident after Monmouth's defeat and execution and was soon on a collision course with Parliament. A certain Judge Jeffreys became notorious in using judicial courts to hang anyone who dared dissent from the king's pro-Catholic views, and his lustful revenge against the defeated Monmouthites earned him the title of 'the hanging judge'. If James had restrained his Catholic ideas, or even emulated his brother's deceit to allay suspicion, he could have united his kingdom without much difficulty. England was in no mood to wage an internal civil war on religious grounds but the tragedy was that James aroused hostility at home and doubts overseas. The doubts came mainly from the Protestant ruler of Holland, William, who had married King James's elder daughter, Mary, and who as the grandson of King Charles the First had an interest in England's affairs that was more than mere academic.

King James and William of Orange were friends for a time but, long before James put on trial seven bishops (including the Archbishop of Canterbury and Bishop of London) for refusing to implement Catholic policy, their friendship had frozen into enmity. Although all the bishops were acquitted, many prominent Englishmen felt that national liberty was in danger and they implored William of Orange, King of Holland (an appointed position nearer to a modern president than an hereditary monarch, known as Stadholder) to invade England and rescue the country from Catholic domination, although in truth King James was foolish rather than tyrannical.

William hesitated when the French promised James help by maintaining an army on the Dutch border. James underlined his stupidity by declining the French offer, claiming he could defend himself without foreign assistance. When the armies of France melted away William set sail; not the expected way across the shortest sea-route but down the English Channel and along the south coast to Brixham, in Devon. Here he could be sure the

Protestants would welcome him. They did; on the highly significant date of 5th November 1688, anniversary of Guy Fawkes's gunpowder plot.

Gathering support *en route*, William marched towards London, 300 miles to the east. Barring his way, at Salisbury, was King James and his trusted military commander John Churchill. Sensing, correctly, the country's mood, Churchill changed sides and his defection broke the nerve of King James. When William of Orange reached London James was still there but was allowed to escape; ensuring there would be no royal blood spilt, no royal martyrs, nor even royal prisoners to provide a focal point for dissenters.

Sometimes called 'The Glorious Revolution' the events of November 1688 were bloodless and gave no-one an excuse for heroics. Very few of the prominent Englishmen who welcomed William as their Protestant saviour and liberator had much idea what his constitutional position would be. If their intention was to offer his wife, Mary, daughter of James the Second, the crown both William and Mary had other ideas. They would agree only to reign together as joint-equals—King William the Third and Queen Mary the Second, always bearing in mind that both William and Mary were not only man and wife but cousins, sharing King Charles the First as their grandfather. She had a warm pleasant personality and was popular throughout England; he was cold, polite but could claim only respect. Moreover he agreed to share the throne only if Parliament would shelve their internal differences and unite in support of himself as king and his wife as queen.

Early in 1689 Parliament met and agreed to invite William and Mary to reign together, with the provision that either would rule alone when their partner died. Assuming they remained childless Mary's sister, Anne, would follow as their successor. This arrangement upset Anne, who resented William's intrusion into a line of succession which had originally placed William after Anne and not before, and she retired from public life in a fit of pique, keeping as her close friends John Churchill and his wife Sarah.

King James might have fled England but he had not abandoned his claim to be the country's king. In France, King Louis XIV gave him the use of a royal palace and encouraged him to try and recover his throne, beginning in the one part of his kingdom where his Catholic views would be most appreciated; Ireland. Early in March, 1689, James landed at Kinsale and met with a warm welcome from the population and resistance from the English army.

The battles fought in Ireland between James and William during 1690 more properly belong to Irish History, especially the significant effect on modern Irish thinking of William's victories at Londonderry and at the River Boyne. 'King Billy'—as William of Orange is known there—and his 'Orangemen' are still remembered as folk heroes in the Protestant communities and are still commemorated annually in parades and demonstrations. It was these defeats in Ireland which effectively ended James's hopes of regaining his throne, especially as French naval power seemed incapable of launching an invasion against the English mainland.

On the continent, King William saw himself as a Protestant bulwark against the growing power of Catholic France, and with forces that were numerically inferior he achieved some victories and endured some losses in a long, bloody campaign that served as a rehearsal for the Duke of Marlborough's series of triumphs during the reign of Queen Anne. In all probability William regarded himself neither as Dutch nor English but as European: he accepted the shared-crown of England with all its restrictions merely to further his great ambition of first curbing and then, if possible, defeating France and so give to Europe its religious freedom.

Parliament had closed ranks to exclude the supporters of James the Second—rabid Catholics who called themselves Jacobites, after *Jacobus* the Latin version of James—and for a brief period William and Mary enjoyed the luxury of a Parliament and people who had sunk their religious and political differences in the common good. Constitutionally, the balance of power had tilted further towards Parliament at the expense of the monarchy. A Bill of Rights ensured the independence of judges and justices of the peace (local magistrates who adjudicate in cases of petty crime); gave individuals the right to petition their king; limited a sovereign's control of the army within England in peacetime and it decreed that Parliament should meet regularly. The Toleration Act enshrined religious freedom and toleration by ending the Protestant Church of England's monopoly of the country's religious life. Anyone was now free to practice their own faith and belief in their own way; yet the act also denied public office to everyone not taking the oath of allegiance to the Protestant king, or not being a member of the Church of England. In other words being an open Catholic automatically resulted in disqualification from all spheres of government.

King William's popularity was never very high and it slumped again when his wife, Queen Mary, died in 1694 and he ruled alone. He developed a close relationship with Hans Bentinck, one of many Dutchmen to hold positions of influence at King William's court, and rumours of a homosexual relationship only added to the king's unpopularity. The fragile unity of Whigs and Tories began to break and William exhausted himself physically and mentally with the effort of leading his army on the continental battlefields and steering Parliament and government into paying for the war. One outcome was the creation in 1694 of the Bank of England which could negotiate loans for the government and regulate the money supply, although it was forbidden to lend the king money without parliamentary approval.

On 8th March 1702 King William died, his poor physical condition giving him no strength to recover from injuries sustained whilst horse-riding. The king's horse stumbled on a mole-hill and threw him off, an incident the Jacobites celebrated annually by raising their glasses every 8th March and toasting 'the black velvet gentleman' meaning the mole that had built the offending molehill.

Queen Anne inherited not only a kingdom but a war, a full-scale international war which was the eighteenth century equivalent of a modern world war.

On 5th September 1701, James the Second had died in France and the French immediately recognised his thirteen year old son, James, as England's lawful king. He is known to history as 'the Old Pretender' and he lived to the age of 79. The attitude of France provoked a renewal of hostilities and a grand alliance of Britain, Austria, Denmark, Holland and the North German States fought against a combination of France, Bavaria and Spain; one issue being French domination of weaker states.

Commander in Chief of the British army was now John Churchill, created Earl of Marlborough by William and further elevated by Queen Anne to be the first Duke of Marlborough. He was destined to be the outstanding man of his age and many historians suggest that he and not Wellington was the greatest military commander ever produced by Great Britain. His wife, the duchess—Sarah—had a tremendous influence over Queen Anne who endured no fewer than seventeen pregnancies into child-birth without any children reaching the age of twelve. The relationship of Anne and Sarah was very close and although the queen was much in love with her dull and stupid husband Prince George of Denmark, she came to rely on Sarah as much for political advice as she relied on Sarah's husband, the duke, for military success. To preserve confidentiality and to give the spice of intrigue to their correspondence, they used *nom de plumes*; Queen Anne signed herself 'Mrs Morley' and the Marlborough's 'Mr and Mrs Freeman'.

In a series of stunning victories, Marlborough beat the French at Blenheim in 1704, at Ramillies in 1706, at Oudenarde in 1708, after which Marlborough and his Austrian ally Prince Eugene invaded France and won another battle at Malplaquet in 1709. Almost every victory was gained against overwhelming odds and none more so than the occasion in August 1711 when Marlborough broke through the French fortified line that stretched from the English Channel into the heart of France, a line reinforced by rivers, canals and any number of ingenious water-barriers. The French called it their Ne Plus Ultra Lines (the 'extremely perfect line' is a rough translation) and Marlborough had to use all his skill and military subtelty to break through.

For the French it was the end and in 1713 the Treaty of Utrecht brought peace; two benefits to England were that Gibraltar became British territory without conditions, and France abandon-ed support for 'the Old Pretender' and instead recognised Queen Anne as the lawful sovereign. The Treaty of Utrecht was lenient to France, mainly because events in England had undermined Marlborough and weakened his intention of exploiting the victories gained by one of the greatest campaigns ever fought under the leadership of a military genius.

Sarah, Duchess of Marlborough, had always been strong-willed and she gave offence all too easily. On 6th April 1710, she and Queen Anne quarrelled violently and they never saw each other again. Sarah and the duke had supported the Whigs, the party which encouraged England's continental war, but with Sarah out of favour the Tory party gained power and sought to negotiate directly with France to end the war. Marlborough was put in an impossible position by his wife's unpopularity with Queen Anne and the political intriguing that followed such domestic quarrels only provoked Whigs and Tories to desert Marlborough just at the moment when the French were in full retreat, diplomatically as well as militarily. With more political unity England could and should have imposed a lasting peace upon Europe. Nevertheless, England had tasted the sweet fruits of victory not only on land but at sea; the naval battle of La Hogue in 1692 had given the Royal Navy a dominance at sea not lost until the mid-twentieth century and it enabled merchants to trade abroad with confidence and an empire to be established world-wide. In every aspects of men's affairs England now held a position centre-stage and had done so whilst giving her subjects religious freedom and a liberty under the law enjoyed by the people of no other European power.

A grateful sovereign and nation rewarded Marlborough by employing Vanbrugh to build for the duke the finest non-royal palace in the world, a palatial residence surrounded by 2,500 acres of landscaped gardens, lakes and parkland; it was called Blenheim Palace after Marlborough's greatest victory. It is still lived-in by the present Duke of Marlborough and was the birthplace in 1874 of another great descendant of the Churchill family; Winston.

The reign of Queen Anne—Marlborough's wars apart—is notable for the way in which party politics began to dominate society in general and Parliament in particular. Sometimes Queen Anne became a passive bystander, as Whigs and Tories debated issues of war and peace and decided policy between themselves. The queen still presided over her council of ministers and the formation of a government administration was still one of the monarch's duties, but such political appointments had now to be handled with more care and the wishes of both the elected House of Commons and hereditary House of Lords considered.

In 1707 the Act of Union was passed through parliament, effectively uniting England and Scotland under one Parliament representing both countries, although certain peculiarities and differences in Scottish Law were allowed to remain and still remain today. From this moment it is correct and more convenient to say 'British' when referring to natives of England, Wales and Scotland. Ireland was either a colony, an occupied land, or a part of 'Britain' in almost permanent revolt; it all depends on the point of view taken.

The final years of the Stuart's produced Henry Purcell, the finest native-born composer ever, who died young and left a vacuum in English music that the German-born George Frederick Handel would soon fill. Sir Christopher Wren who straddled the era, living to the age of ninety, handing on a tradition of architecture to his pupils Hawksmoor and Vanbrugh. Wren himself lived to see the completion of his undoubted masterpiece, St Paul's Cathedral, in 1710, and its official consecration that year gave Queen Anne the opportunity to have her statue in the place of honour outside the impressive west entrance. In the literary world, newspapers made their first appearance, creating an appetite for the printed word filled by Daniel Defoe (Robinson Crusoe), Jonathan Swift (Gulliver's Travels) and William Congreve who wrote some of the most irreverent and witty plays to grace the English theatre.

On 1st August 1714 Queen Anne died childless, the last Stuart sovereign. Her multiple pregnancies and constant ill-health had afforded her few chances to dominate national affairs. Her reign had brought political stability at home and military prestige abroad, and although it was her good fortune to have in John Churchill a military commander brilliant enough to hide her own lack of leadership, it was her equal misfortune for that same man to have as his wife, Sarah, a woman whose political ineptitude helped neither her husband, her queen nor her country.

10

When Queen Anne died in 1714 the country we now call Germany was a fragmentation of small self-governing states, the most northerly of which was Hanover. Ruled by a king called George—the Hanoverians called him an Elector—at fifty-four years of age he was no longer considered young. George and Queen Anne shared King James the First as their mutual great-grandfather, George's mother Sophie being the daughter of Elizabeth of Bohemia, who in turn was the daughter of James the First and sister to Charles the First. Thus George, a German by birth and temperament, succeeded to the throne of England by a most indirect route.

The Act of Succession passed by Parliament in 1701 anticipated that King William the Third and Queen Anne might die childless as had Charles the Second, and in order to exclude all non-protestants from the line of succession the Act decreed that the descendants of Elizabeth of Bohemia would ascend the throne. It is this Act which gives our present sovereign the legal right to rule. The Divine Right of Kings had given way to an Act which made Parliament supreme.

King George the First arrived in England on 29th September 1714, a grey foggy day that forced his sailing ship to anchor before reaching the welcoming reception at Greenwich, and he completed the final stage of his journey by undignified rowing boat. In the baroque splendour of Sir Christopher Wren's Royal Naval Hospital at Greenwich is a mural depicting the king's arrival and adjoining it is a much larger wall-painting of George the First and his royal family in all their glory; over the group reads a Latin inscription: Iam Nova Progenies Coelo (Now there is a new race in heaven).

The new race of Hanoverians as represented by King George was very Germanic; stolid, coarse-humoured, but appreciative of good music. Especially opera and the compositions of George Frederick Handel, who had paid a brief visit to England in the reign of Queen Anne but who now took up permanent residence under the royal patronage of King George. England's new king brought his son, Prince George, with him but not his wife who had earlier been divorced and was destined to spend the final twenty-two years of her life in prison. Her place had been taken by a number of mistresses of which two became ensconced within the English court: Charlotte Sophie Kielmannsegge, who was fat and dumpy, and Ehrengard Melusina von Schulenburg, who was tall and slender. Englishmen quickly dubbed them 'the elephant and the maypole'. Prince George and his father had developed a mutual distrust for each other that ripened into outright enmity, starting a tradition of unfortunate father/son relationships that pervaded the royal family until King George the Sixth ascended the throne in 1936.

Not surprisingly, Protestant King George favoured Protestant Whigs to form his government, even though Whigs frequently quarrelled with each other and their disunity made leading the party difficult. The pro-Jacobite Tories were soon in eclipse when they voiced support for 'the Old Pretender' who, in 1715, landed in Scotland from France calling himself King James the Third. The revolt he led was small-scale and easily crushed before the disturbance could spread to England. Nevertheless, King George was obliged to execute two noblemen for their part in the Scottish uprising, causing some Whigs to accuse the king of being too lenient. But the Whigs were now in firm political control and were destined to remain in power for forty-eight unbroken years.

For a time King George took an interest in English politics, enjoying the flattery of wealthy aristocrats who vied with each other to gain the king's support for their own especial point of view. Gambling, womanising and music were George the First's main interests but he disliked the pomp and ceremonial expected from him and he soon made plans to return to his beloved Hanover where he could rule his German subjects autocratically without the hindrance and restrictions of a Parliament. This led to the problem of allowing Prince George to remain in England with the traditional power and responsibility of acting in the king's place. King George could speak some English but when he presided at meetings with his ministers Prince George sat by his father's side and translated where necessary. Not only did the king resent this dependency, he wanted to avoid giving his son the opportunity of presiding at such meetings during the king's frequent absences.

The solution, quite by chance, was a further step in the evolution of English democracy. For several years senior ministers had regular meetings presided over by the reigning sovereign, and because they were originally held in a small room, or cabinet, they became known as Cabinet Meetings. The most important minister was then First Lord of the Treasury and he was now authorised to preside at Cabinet Meetings and thus exclude the king, and the king's son. Although still regarded as 'first among equals', he was, nevertheless, 'first minister' or Prime Minister; even now British Prime Ministers hold the title of First Lord of the Treasury in addition to that of Prime Minister. Sir Robert Walpole was the first beneficiary of this new arrangement and he took full advantage of his new position. Walpole reformed the machinery of governing the country, making Cabinets jointly responsible for the decisions, as ministers, they took together. He also made sure that the elected House of Commons would be pre-eminent over the hereditary House of Peers. For a full twenty years, from 1721 to 1741, Sir Robert Walpole remained as Prime Minister, although he continued to pay as much attention to his farm in Norfolk as he did to affairs of state. He pursued two main objectives and was largely successful in them both: the first was to keep England at peace during a time when war waged from one end of the continent to the other. The second objective was to restore financial stability to England after the infamous South Sea Bubble of 1720.

William the Third's successful creation in 1694 of the Bank of England was dominated by Whigs and gave them political and financial power. In 1711 a group of Tories created a rival institution to give themselves a degree of political and financial influence. Forming the South Sea Company they contracted to take responsibility for part of the national debt in return for a monopoly of trade with South America; hence the name of their company. At first the venture was a success and in 1720 the company increased their debt responsibility from ten million pounds to forty million pounds. Thousands of investors poured money into the company and, in a rash of enterprise, began capital schemes on the strength of anticipated rich profits.

Within a year it was all over. The bubble burst and brought financial ruin to a whole range of individuals, ministers and companies. Sir Robert Walpole emerged unscathed from the taint of corruption that had destroyed the political careers of Whigs who had invested unwisely, and to restore financial stability he began a programme of taxation and levying custom duty on tobacco, wine and spirits that encouraged an orgy of smuggling and made him the most unpopular man in Britain. Nevertheless, Walpole ignored the criticism and became the most outstanding politician of his day. He was above corruption and when he was offered a house in London he accepted it, but only on behalf of all future Prime Ministers who still use it as their London residence; Number Ten, Downing Street.

In 1727 King George the First died in Germany and his son was duly crowned King George the Second. The transition caused barely a ripple on the surface of English political and social life, nothing had changed: the enmity between father and son transferred itself to England's new king and son, Prince Frederick, and Sir Robert Walpole continued in office as Prime Minister, serving the new king as he had the old.

This was a period in which politics and politicians were held in low esteem by the working classes, few of whom owned the minimum property necessary to give them a vote in elections, making parliamentary democracy something of a sham by modern standards. Sons of the aristocracy or country gentlemen (squires) were usually elected to the House of Commons and they frequently regarded themselves as members of an undemanding club where they could enjoy the social stimulation of living for short periods in London.

Grand houses and villas in the Italian Palladian style reflected the prosperity of farmers and merchants. Many housed small libraries and modest art-collections acquired on cultural tours to Italy and beyond. Painters with the taste and stature of Thomas Gainsborough and Joshua Reynolds would record for posterity the grace and elegance of life in eighteenth-century England, whilst at the same time Handel's music gave a splendour to the ceremonial of church and state and the theatre flourished as never before, with John Gay's *The Beggar's Opera* becoming a real landmark. The English novel was born when Henry Fielding wrote *Tom Jones* and Laurence Sterne followed with *Tristram Shandy*, books that ladies and gentlemen of leisure had the time to read and intelligence to understand. Such elegant spa towns as Bath and Harrogate were created as resorts for those who were sick—or thought to be sick; places in which to drink the medicinal waters by day and luxuriate in uplifting concerts and theatrical plays by night. Courtesy and good manners assumed an exaggerated importance it is now all too easy to parody but which, at the time, mirrored the age of refinement and formality.

Unfortunately, this wealth and general prosperity benefited only the upper echelons of society. Labourers and household servants were poorly rewarded for their long hours of work and, although no-one starved, the gulf between rich and poor widened throughout each reign of the first four Georges. Nevertheless there was little resentment and no class hatred. Bad though conditions were for the English working classes they were still superior to their continental counterparts, who felt that only a violent overthrow of the existing regime could change things.

Slowly and painfully, Sir Robert Walpole guided his country into national prosperity, ignoring the caustic attacks made on him by newspapers and magazines seeking a more adventurous approach to foreign policy. Walpole's proud boast of keeping England out of war was not universally popular. To be at peace, and advantageously prosperous, when France and her Spanish ally were rampaging across Europe seemed to be an affront to the sacrifices England had made during Marlborough's Wars and many found this utterly shameful. In time the war-mongers would have their way.

During 1739, an English sea-captain, Robert Jenkins, aroused public indignation when he declared that Spaniards had cut off his ear in a trade dispute on the high seas. Against his better-judgement Walpole was obliged to declare war and when he heard church bells pealing out their call to arms he observed to a friend: 'Now they are ringing their bells; soon they will be wringing their hands'. The 'War of Jenkins' Ear', as it became known, was not a success and Walpole lost office. His lasting achievement was to consolidate parliamentary and monarchial power and establish the Cabinet as the means of putting Parliament's wishes into executive action. It was unspectacular but of inestimable value in the context of British history. His son, Horace Walpole, was to become an arbiter of taste, reviving the gothic tradition and incorporating it into domestic architecture which bears the name of his house built in that style; Strawberry Hill Gothic.

King George the Second's hostility towards his son, Prince Frederick, heightened the tension and latent instability of English politics. Prince Frederick repeated what his father had done to George the First; establish a rival court in London and make it a focal point for dissident politicians opposed to the king and his ministers. Even George the Second's wife, Queen Caroline, who was generally popular, made her hatred of Prince Frederick so public and so venemous that the prince and his political friend gained much sympathy. Having ousted Walpole and embarked on a war against France, it was necessary for the country to find a leader who could bring some sort of victory to England—not only on the continent, where the British struggled to halt French advances but also in Canada and India where our traders were being harassed by rival French forces.

For a time no leader with the stature of Walpole emerged and Britain continued to flounder against the better-organised French. Taking advantage of yet another British defeat, this time at Fontenoy in Holland, France encouraged the 'Old Pretender's' son, Prince Charles Edward Stuart, to invade England and regain the crown lost by his great-grandfather King James the Second in 1688. Bonnie Prince Charlie, as he is popularly known, landed in Scotland during 1745 and immediately incited a rebellion against the Hanoverian English, just as his father had done in 1715. Bonnie

Prince Charlie had a much more charismatic personality and he took advantage of the traditional grievances felt by many Scots against the English.

Gathering support, he crossed the border into England and advanced 200 miles south as far as Derby, meeting only token resistance. Then, as if afraid of the consequences of actually winning, Bonnie Prince Charlie inexplicably turned north again and drifted back towards Scotland bewildering his supporters and making little attempt to secure his line of retreat. George the Second took full advantage and despatched his loyal son the Duke of Cumberland to crush the insurrection. Earning the title Butcher Cumberland, he employed a ruthless brutality that is still remembered in Scotland today, destroying both the clan system and the long-cherished independence of the Scottish highlands. Culloden, near Inverness, became the site of a battle that degenerated into a massacre when Bonnie Prince Charlie's supporters met their final defeat, although the last Stuart prince escaped to France and oblivion with the help of a brave Scots girl, Flora Macdonald.

Walpole could not go on for ever and a number of aristocratic Whigs became Prime Minister in turn, all of them lacking vision and honest competence. However one of them, the Duke of Devonshire, almost reluctantly, under pressure, persuaded the king to appoint as Secretary of State the man who seemed capable of restoring British pride in their struggle with France; he was William Pitt, a persistent critic of weak government policy. His friendship with Prince Frederick was enough in itself to ensure the king's displeasure. Nevertheless, Pitt had ideas that commanded popular support and he was not lacking in self-confidence, boldly asserting: 'I can save this country and nobody else can'. Pitt was applauded by the labouring classes and bankers alike as he demonstrated many times that he had a clear view of what was happening abroad and where Britain's friends and enemies could be found. His policies met with success at once, in North America, India, Europe and on the high seas. During the four years from 1756 to 1760 he changed the balance of power throughout the western world.

India came first: Since Elizabethan times the East India Company had been trading there not as a colony on virgin territory, but as merchants with Indian consent. Trading centres had been established in Bombay, Madras and Bengal competing with the French on equal terms. However in 1707 the Muslim ruler died—the Great Mogul—and the vacuum he left began to be filled by the French, who saw an opportunity to control all India and exclude the English. During Walpole's term of office the French had succeeded but now a young man in the East India Company started to reverse everything that had gone before. Robert Clive—Clive of India—out-fought and out-manoeuvred the French, achieving his greatest victory at the Battle of Plassey. From that moment Britain, and not France, became the dominant European voice on the Indian sub-continent.

It was a similar story in North America and especially in Canada: Newfoundland and Nova Scotia (New Scotland) had been declared British spheres of influence after the 1713 Treaty of Utrecht which resulted from Marlborough's defeat of the French. English colonies had already been established but were being challenged by the forces of France: Pitt chose a young officer, Major-General James Wolfe, to regain the initiative. At the Heights of Abraham, by a brilliant combination of the army and Royal Navy, Wolfe defeated his French rival and captured Quebec. He died during the battle but his brilliant tactics were enough to earn him immortality and his well-trained army pursued the retreating French army south through the Ohio valley and by so doing eliminated all French opposition from North America; Fort Duquesne was renamed Pittsburgh in honour of William Pitt, architect of the campaign that had made all British colonies on the North American continent secure.

Yet more successes were recorded in the West Indies and on Continental Europe. Pitt had shrewdly made the arrangement with Frederick the Great that his Prussian army would fight the French on land and the British navy fight them at sea and elsewhere abroad. Unfortunately, King Frederick was unable to prevent the French from threatening Hanover itself—homeland of George the Second who had also succeeded to the title and duties of Elector of Hanover—but Pitt saved the situation by a timely despatch of well-trained soldiers who defeated a numerically-superior French army at the Battle of Minden.

As if to crown Pitt's achievements, in that same year of 1759 the Royal Navy scored a spectacular victory off the coast of Brittany which was enough by itself to end all hopes of French expansionism. This was 'the glorious year' to which David Garrick referred in his patriotic song 'Hearts of Oak', the unofficial anthem of the Royal Navy from that day to this.

On 25th October 1760, at the age of seventy-six, King George the Second died, his reign ending in a blaze of glory with Britain everywhere supreme both militarily and economically. The king's grandson, a third George, now succeeded to the throne; his father Prince Frederick having died in 1751.

King George the Third was just twenty-two years old and immature for his age. Tall and physically attractive, he had the same lusty desire for women as the first two Georges. Announcing that as a duty to his kingdom he would marry and produce heirs, he agreed to marry a German princess without even seeing her. She was Princess Charlotte from the tiny state of Strelitz (now part of East Germany) and although everyone judged her exceedingly plain, she was married to the king the very same day she arrived in London. It was a happy marriage producing no fewer than nine sons and six daughters, many of them born in the modest house that became a favourite residence of Queen Charlotte, Buckingham House; this would later be extended by her eldest son, George the Fourth, into the sovereign's main London home, Buckingham Palace.

Having achieved his first priority of a suitable marriage, George the Third turned his attention to politics and revealed his ambition to take more power into his own hands. The king probably had no desire to revert back to the Stuart concept of the Divine Right of Kings but he did feel Georges One and Two had allowed their royal prerogative to be eroded in favour of their newly created Prime Ministers. George set out to reverse this trend and for the next twenty years or more he ruled by taking very little notice of the quarrelling Whigs and discredited Jacobite Tories; in effect he created his own political party and they commanded a majority within Parliament.

William Pitt and his ally the Duke of Newcastle were soon dismissed from office. Pitt, notwithstanding his great triumphs in defeating the French, had never found favour with the Whigs and he was detested by King George the Third who disliked on principle every minister who had served George the Second. The king now appointed his one-time tutor and personal confidant the Earl of Bute as Prime Minister, and he negotiated a peace treaty with France which, although it formally ceded Canada to Britain was as foolishly lenient as that following Marlborough's War fifty years earlier.

Bute had neither parliamentary experience nor political skill and he soon became exceedingly unpopular. King George quickly replaced him by an arrogant Whig, George Grenville, who proved equally ineffective and in rapid succession the king appointed one Prime Minister after another. William Pitt was not among them. He suffered from acute ill-health all his life, although he frequently confounded his opponents by recovering from severe attacks of gout to lambast the government's ineptitude that was driving the American colonists towards rebellion which Pitt knew could be averted. The real tragedy was that Pitt the Elder (his son, also William, and also to be Prime Minister during a time of crisis we call Pitt the Younger) lacked the gift of making political friends and paying compliments to his king. His prestige and great influence came from his leadership in the successful war against France, his fine oratory inside Parliament, and widespread support among the general public who recognised common sense when they heard it; however in an age without a powerful media this was not enough. King George grudgingly elevated Pitt the Elder to become Earl of Chatham but in the coming debate to decide the fate of America Pitt would be no more than an articulate critic of muddled governmental policy. This was an age of corruption by inefficient ministers, of political instability, and of a king who meddled in a parliamentary system he did not understand. It was also a time of great social change.

The war recently ended with France had fuelled a demand for ships, guns, clothing and all the requirements to sustain an army and navy. This upsurge in manufacture proved to be the midwife for a new kind of production inspired by Adam Smith, author of the influential book *The Wealth of Nations*. This concentrated work in large factories rather than small workshops. James Hargreaves had invented the Spinning Jenny—a machine to spin thread—and Sir Thomas Arkwright had developed this into a Spinning Frame, building a factory to mass-produce textiles for the first time. In order to carry raw material from seaports to inland towns a network of canals were built and horse-drawn barges became a familiar sight almost everywhere. Roads were being improved, and in time John McAdam's invention of making an inexpensive surface of stones bonded by tar (macadam roads) would enable an increasing number of fast stagecoaches to overcome the difficulties of terrain and thieving highwaymen to criss-cross the country with a regular and reliable service linking all major towns and cities.

This social change brought few benefits to the working classes, other than a longer life and more varied diet due to the introduction from abroad of new types of fruit and vegetables. The gulf between rich and poor widened further when food prices increased as a result of poor harvests. Armed mobs roamed the streets, inflamed with violence by the rabble-rouser John Wilkes: for a time there was even a smell of revolution in the air which evaporated as quickly as it came.

King George's appointment of Lord North as Prime Minister in 1770 certainly helped in stabilising matters. North cared little for personal popularity and slowly the country resumed an even tenor in the wake of better harvests and a king who began to work hard and successfully at mastering the art of ruling his kingdom. Parliament, government and sovereign were equally concerned in persuading American colonists to pay for their own defence and contribute towards the expensive war waged by Pitt to secure their independence from the French. Every attempt to impose even modest taxation met with civil disobedience and a blank refusal from colonists who still maintained loyalty towards their king, George the Third, but not towards the king's government. Their argument was that they had no voice in England's Parliament thousands of miles away, and 'No taxation without representation' became the universal cry of defiance.

Parliament had been shrewd in imposing taxes only on those goods that could not be produced in America, levying a rate of taxation much lower than that prevailing in England. Tea was one such product and when, in December 1773, the people of Boston threw a cargo of tea overboard rather than pay tax on it there was an immediate confrontation. The British Parliament declared various trade sanctions against their American cousins who in turn grew ever more resentful. Sporadic acts of violence flared between the British red-coats and American colonists, until in April 1775 this developed into a full-scale battle in and around Boston, leading to an uprising up and down the American colonies.

Samuel Johnson—the 'Great Doctor Johnson'—was not only a memorable literary critic, creator of the first true English diction-ary and patron of David Garrick the actor and patriotic song-writer, he was also one of the many Englishmen who were intent on humbling the rebel colonists. In this regard King George and Lord North were reflecting popular sentiment by their North American policy.

For a time British soldiers were successful, their training and discipline overcoming American enthusiasm and determination. At this stage a political settlement might have been possible but when, on 4th July 1776, the Americans declared their indepen-dance and specifically denied loyalty to George the Third, their lawful king, there was no room for compromise on either side.

General George Washington, who had once served in the British Army, led his fellow-colonists with a stubborn persistence that took full advantage of the long coastline and broad inland territory that proved impossible for the British to conquer and occupy. Surviving the harsh winter of 1776-1777, Washington moved onto the offensive and on 17th October 1777 achieved a victory which almost certainly ensured Britain could not win the war. General John Burgoyne (known as 'Gentleman Johnny') surrendered his British army of 6,000 men to his American opponent, General Horatio Gates, at Saratoga and this had the effect of persuading the French to seize their opportunity and enter the war side by side with America. Holland followed France's example and from that moment Britain could only lose a war they should never have begun. Half the western world had taken the side of America against England and almost everyone but King George now realised the war was over.

Nevertheless, for a further five years, from the Canadian border to South Carolina, the battles spluttered like a fire that was refusing to be extinguished. Then, in 1782, due to a skilful naval blockade, George Washington forced the remaining British force, under their commander Lord Cornwallis, to surrender at Yorkstown. The war had ended in bitter humiliation for Great Britain and, in September 1783, the French and Americans confirmed their success when they forced Britain to sign a peace treaty in Paris which granted to an independent America everything the British had tried to deny them.

America was gracious and magnanimous in her hour of triumph and quickly sent John Adams to London as America's first official ambassador where he was warmly received by King George the Third. Thus a spirit of goodwill and mutual generosity that has stood the test of time was born, broken only by the mere hiccup of a short naval war in 1812. The long and happy Anglo-American special relationship had begun.

France was soon to realise that her part in Britain's humiliation was no more than a Pyrrhic victory for which a heavy price was about to be exacted. No doubt inspired by America's successful rebellion the French rose to overthrow their own monarch in the revolutionary bloodbath of 1789.

In England the political repercussions of defeat were almost as traumatic and King George became exposed as the architect of governmental incompetence. The House of Commons was determined to reassert its control over national policy and voted decisively in favour of the resolution: 'The influence of the Crown has increased, is increasing, and ought to be diminished'. Instead of a bloody revolution, political democracy found its solution in the reintroduction of two-party politics and a general election designed to give the House of Commons a new voice.

The Whigs were now led by the unlikely combination of Lord North and a radical with anti-royalist views; Charles James Fox. So strong were his ideas that Fox was sometimes called 'Oliver Cromwell the Second', although his libertine views were most unpuritan. The Tories were led by William Pitt's son, also called William but known to history as Pitt the Younger, becoming Prime Minister at the early age of twenty-four. Supported by King

George he won the 1784 election by a huge margin, trouncing Lord North and Fox into political oblivion. Fox, however, now mellowed into a radical humanitarian and formed an alliance with the arch-Tory and Pitt supporter, William Wilberforce, and together these two combined to force Britain into abandoning slavery when almost every other country was exploiting the blacks of Africa and the Caribbean to create a vast army of negro slaves. It was Wilberforce and Fox who, by their oratory, pricked the conscience of Britain and persuaded the abolition of slavery to be adopted as official governmental policy.

As Britain grasped the nettle of freeing the slaves, France began to spread the seeds of revolution across Europe. Napoleon Bonaparte seemed poised to conquer not only Europe but Africa and Asia too, so that for a time the threat of continental invasion caused Britain to renew her coastal defences for the first time in over a century.

Pitt and his Tories grew increasingly nervous when there were suggestions that Parliament should reform itself to make it more responsive to a wider voting population. This was interpreted as 'back-door-revolution' and Pitt the Younger responded by banning all public meetings and disbanding the new working class groups called Trade Unions. Only the good sense of some independently-minded judges defused an explosive situation when charges were brought against men who tried to insist on their traditional English freedoms.

George the Third was now a passive observer as the European crisis deepened. He had suffered from ill-health most of his life and by 1788 was physically deteriorating. He was thought to be mad and for a time had to be restrained in a strait-jacket, being much abused by his doctors, who were in ignorance of the true reason behind the king's illness. Modern medical science would have diagnosed this as porphyria and effected a cure; nevertheless for many generations afterwards the king has been unjustly derided as being mentally unbalanced. King George was destined to live to a ripe old age but it was an unhappy and pitiable existence into which he drifted, virtually a prisoner in Windsor Castle, enjoying only brief spells of lucidity.

Pitt the Younger had even greater problems than personal ill-health to contend with. French revolutionaries had executed their own king and queen, together with most of the aristocracy of France. Now they declared their intention of supporting any rebellion in Europe and began to threaten once again the weaker states of Holland and Germany. In 1793 Pitt decided to 'save Europe' and so launched into another conflict between England and France that continued for over twenty years.

Battles were fought in two main areas initially. First of all the West Indies; just as his father had secured Canada by promoting a combined naval force supporting a well-trained army, so Pitt the Younger attempted a similar venture in the Caribbean. Unfortunately, tropical diseases ran riot and withdrawal was impossible; 40,000 British soldiers died in three years, adding very little of any substance to the British Empire, although French influence in the area had been greatly reduced.

Secondly, on the high seas, Pitt was more successful. For some time both ships and men had been in a poor state of readiness but on 1st August 1798 the Royal Navy proved itself to be in good shape again. Napoleon Bonaparte had captured Malta, had appeared to be in control of the Mediterranean Sea, and was now poised to attack both Turkey and India. A rising naval officer, Horatio Nelson, revealed his skill and tactical judgement in attacking and defeating the French fleet in an action we call The Battle of the Nile. If Saratoga had been a turning point in one war, the Nile was equally important in another, securing British naval supremacy in the trade routes through Mediterranean waters.

Pitt the Younger, lacked the flair and sure-footedness of his father but he displayed his far-sighted attitude and strategic thinking when he declared: 'England has saved herself by her exertions; and will, I trust, save Europe by her example'. With Holland desperately protecting her own borders, Austria beaten and helpless by 1797, and Spain allied with Napoleonic France, Great Britain faced an uncertain future as the Eighteenth Century gave way to the Nineteenth.

11

NELSON AND WELLINGTON (1800 to 1837)

Even among the great English heroes Horatio Nelson is rather special, a man to be loved not merely admired. It is impossible to exaggerate the adulation given to him during his lifetime by the general public and he still remains to us a very warm and human figure.

Few men are given Nelson's opportunity and genius to change the course of world history. Even fewer do so whilst unhappily married and conducting an indiscreet love-affair with the wife of a high-ranking diplomat. To achieve fame and glory and at the same time gain a well-deserved reputation for kindness and benevolence is rare indeed.

Nelson seems an improbable hero. Born in 1758, the son of a rural clergyman, he was educated at a school within the shadow of Norwich Cathedral where he grew exceedingly fond of Shakespeare and other classics. Although frail and physically short in stature he joined the Royal Navy as a midshipman when he was twelve, showing personal courage and a capacity to disregard orders. Even so he gained rapid promotion and his devotion to the sailors under him secured their abiding respect and affection, especially when he lost an arm and an eye in two separate naval battles. Nelson's habitual seasickness only added to his popularity and made him appear more human and less remote to his men. He was already a public idol when he fell in love with Emma, the wife of Sir William Hamilton who at that time was King George's Ambassador to the King of Naples. Nelson and Emma made no secret of their passion for each other and the general public enjoyed the romantic spectacle of a great national hero in love with a beautiful and tempestuous young woman. Sir William was understanding and created few difficulties; Nelson's wife was less accommodating and showed her bitterness and anger at every opportunity.

If Nelson's private life was something of a mess it merely served to add spice to his sense of duty and patriotism as a sailor who gave every indication of saving England single-handed. At one time the threat of invasion from France's Napoleon Bonaparte was very real and evidence of the coastal defences thought to be necessary during this period can still be seen along the south coast of England. However Nelson gave England control of the sea and denied France any opportunity to invade this country or to expand the French Empire anywhere but on continental Europe.

William Pitt, as Prime Minister, was shrewd enough to appreciate Nelson's ability even as a junior officer and England reaped the benefit. The Battle of the Nile stopped Napoleon's advance on the high seas and soon afterwards Nelson destroyed the Danish fleet at the Battle of Copenhagen and this effectively neutralised both Scandinavia and Russia, preventing them from joining forces with France. From that moment the Royal Navy was in control of all international waters as Nelson chased the French navy back to their home ports, until in the autumn of 1805 the combined French and Spanish fleets under the command of Admiral Villeneuve left Cadiz and were intercepted by Nelson's numerically inferior fleet close to Cape Trafalgar.

As a strategist and naval tactician, Horatio Nelson stands supreme. With the confidence of his junior officers who worshipped him—The Band of Brothers he called them—Nelson deployed his ships with great skill, using their guns to maximum effect. With his own ship HMS Victory leading the way, he sent the famous signal that every Englishman knows by heart: 'England Expects that Every Man will do his Duty'. The ensuing Battle of Trafalgar was a spectacular success. The French fleet was destroyed, Admiral Villeneuve captured, yet although no British ship was lost the Royal Navy grieved and mourned a loss greater than any fleet of ships: Nelson was dead.

Courageous and careless of his own personal safety, he remained on deck, in full uniform wearing all his glittering decorations. Almost inevitably an alert French sniper took full advantage and shot a musket ball into Nelson, shattering his spine. His last words to Thomas Hardy, Captain of the *Victory*, have a pathos that can move men still: 'Kiss me Hardy. Now I am satisfied. Thank God, I have done my duty'. He lived just long enough after the battle to know details of the total victory he had planned so carefully, although unaware that it would be the last great battle fought between wooden sailing ships before the evolution of iron-clad steam-driven battleships. His funeral under the dome of St Paul's Cathedral was the signal for a nation to express its grief at losing a hero who was valiant, noble, and beloved all at once. His ship HMS *Victory* is now preserved in Portsmouth dockyard, a place of pilgrimage for sailors of all nations. On the anniversary of Nelson's last sea-battle, 21st October, a naval parade takes place in London's Trafalgar Square and many Royal Navy ships hold a commemorative dinner, at which the toast is drunk not to Nelson by name but to 'The Immortal Memory'. Nelson died a revered hero at the age of forty-six, his immortal memory untainted by subsequent political adventures, something which happened to the Duke of Wellington, who continued on land what Nelson had achieved at sea.

Nelson had been created a Viscount but did not live long enough to climb higher up the aristocratic ladder. Arthur Wellesley, coming from an Irish family with musical rather than military traditions, in due time was elevated to the highest rank open to those of non-royal birth, a dukedom, and it is as Duke of Wellington that Arthur Wellesley is known to history.

Europe after Trafalgar was in effect blockaded by the Royal Navy, and trading between continental countries and the rest of the world came to an end. America resented British warships interferring with their commercial interests and a short naval war in 1812 soured Anglo-American relations for a time. Trafalgar also revealed a weakness between France and Spain and it was this which Wellington began to exploit. Using Portugal—England's oldest ally—as a springboard, the British landed an army there under the command of General Sir John Moore. Moore was the army's nearest equivalent to Nelson and he used his army with great wisdom until being killed at Corunna; there he was buried amidst much personal sorrowing by the soldiers he loved and who returned his love in full measure. The incident inspired Charles Wolfe to write the poem beginning: *Not a drum was heard, not a funeral note, As his corpse to the rampart we hurried; Not a soldier discharged his farewell shot Over the grave where our hero we buried.* And ending: *Slowly and sadly we laid him down, From the field of his fame, fresh and gory; We carved not a line, and we raised not a stone, But we left him alone with his glory.*

Wellington now took advantage of what Sir John Moore had begun, driving the French army back across the Pyrenee Mountains into their own territory. As a military genius Wellington can be compared only with Marlborough in the previous century. Both fought the French on Continental Europe and pitted British forces against an army numerically greater, and both were aware of fighting a tyrant bent on subduing smaller and weaker states. Wellington organised his men into a truly efficient military machine, advancing or standing his ground in lines abreast where their firepower could be used to advantage against the French columns. In defence he organised his soldiers into 'squares' where, with some kneeling and others standing, the square of riflemen defied the opposing cavalry with a devastating fire-power from every angle. Other Europeans grasped their opportunity to emulate the British redcoats and surged into France, free at last from the myth of French invincibility which had already been exposed in 1812 when the Russian winter forced Napoleon to make his long retreat from the gates of Moscow.

Napoleon Bonaparte was now exiled to Elba and a brief peace descended on Europe until he escaped and returned to France, raising his standard of war again. England felt the need to stop Napoleon once more and despatched Wellington to Flanders at the head of a modestly-sized army. A few miles from Brussels, on 18th June 1815, Wellington braced his men to meet Napoleon near the village of Waterloo. Wellington's victory was so crushing, so decisive, that 'Waterloo' has become an alternative name for such a massively over-whelming victory. In fairness it must be stated that Wellington was in some danger until Blucher and his Prussian army arrived on the scene to make the outcome safe. As Wellington himself admitted 'it was a close-run thing!' Waterloo certainly ensured the reputation of Wellington's best troops, the guards, the 'thin red line' he called them, and was once heard to remark: 'I don't know what effect these men have on an enemy but by God they terrify me!'

With Napoleon Bonaparte defeated, discredited, and securely exiled on the island of St Helena in mid-Atlantic, a conference was held in Austria to divide the spoils of war and dismantle the French empire. Pitt the Younger had died in 1806 exhausted by reconciling the opposing factions in Ireland and by promoting the cause of defeating Napoleon in a Parliament that had a powerful anti-war element eager to condemn the cost of victory. Viscount Castelreagh and Wellington therefore represented England at the 1815 Congress of Vienna and ensured their country was adequately rewarded for saving Europe. Accordingly, several important island outposts such as Malta and Corfu, hitherto controlled by France, came under British rule.

The Royal Navy now had an endless chain of stations around the world from which the rapidly expanding British Empire could be defended and trade routes secured. Ever since the American colonies had been lost a second empire had been emerging, due mainly to the voyages of discovery by Captain James Cook. Australia, New Zealand and a whole string of useful islands in the Pacific were now planted with the British flag and joined India, Canada and various enclaves around the coast of Africa as 'an empire on which the sun never sets'. This empire would, in time, create an opportunity for Englishmen—and, particularly in Canada, Scotsmen too—to settle on virgin territory, taking with them a desire to escape from an overcrowded island, yet retaining their respect for a constitutional monarchy and that taste for law-abiding liberty that has so characterised the people of this country since Magna Carta was sealed.

For liberating Europe from Napoleon the nation benefited in prestige and the addition of territory overseas, but as individuals the people paid a heavy price. Income Tax to pay for the war had been invented, an industrial economy based on supplying the military had been created and then allowed to lose its impetus when victory came in sight, resulting in much unemployment. The rising birthrate was already bringing problems as England's agricultural labourers surged into overcrowded cities looking for work. In 1819 a mass meeting of disenchanted workers demanding the right to vote was held in St Peter's Field, Manchester. The meeting was dispersed by a ruthless cavalry charge from the local military garrison and although only eleven people were killed the incident became known as The Peterloo Massacre; a word-play on the scene of Wellington's great victory four years earlier. Peterloo served to make parliamentary reform more urgent and it probably influenced the creation of a police force to maintain law and order, rather than entrust this duty to the military. Sir Robert Peel, in 1829, established the Metropolitan Police Force, since which time they have been known as 'Bobbies'.

Parliamentary reform was less easy to achieve. The government of the day was inclined to be repressive and reactionary, mindful of the 1792 French Revolution. Parliament further inflamed popular opinion when the land-owning majority passed the Corn Law to prevent the importation of cheap grain. Similar measures were taken to keep out goods produced less-expensively overseas and whilst the argument over Free Trade raged as an academic issue, the country's population suffered real hardship due to lack of work, insanitary housing within cities, and prices held artificially high to protect factory-owners and wealthy farmers.

Leading the opposition to any reform was the great Duke of Wellington who entered politics, becoming Prime Minister in 1828. This is where his reputation and Nelson's differ. Both were military leaders who won glorious victories to massive public acclaim and rejoicing but Nelson died in the service of his country and remains the quintessence of a national hero; Wellington is remembered by posterity as a reactionary politician who shuttered the windows of his house to protect them from the stone-throwing mob; an act that earned him the title 'The Iron Duke'.

Nevertheless, Wellington or no Wellington, Parliament could not resist the pressure for change as outlined in the Great Charter of 1832. This proposed that all householders paying a yearly rent of £10 would have the right to vote in national elections and that the 'rotten boroughs' which produced unrepresentative Members of Parliament from a small number of electors would be consolidated into fewer constituencies with more voters. The largely middle-class House of Commons approved the Charter, the land-owning House of Lords rejected it until the king (William the Fourth) put pressure on Wellington and his friends to ensure the Great Charter was passed by both Houses of Parliament. After new elections based on the Reform Bill (or Great Charter) a whole series of Acts of Parliament to benefit the poor came into being. Sir Robert Peel became Prime Minister and his Tories began to be known by their modern name of Conservatives.

Slavery was abolished in all British territories overseas, at a cost of twenty million pounds in compensation to slave-owners. A system of education for every child in the country was begun and money provided by Parliament for this purpose. The Earl of Shaftesbury introduced the first Factory Act to regulate working conditions in factories and limit child-labour in such places. Relief to help the poor was provided and although conditions in many 'workhouses' (in effect hostels offering shelter to the homeless) were abysmal, it was at least a recognition that some degree of help was needed. Administrative machinery was created to make town councils elected by local tax-payers and so these councils would now be responsible for local services to benefit the local community.

England had not suddenly transformed itself into Utopia but the Reform Bill had established a more representative Parliament, which could respond to the social conditions in a changing society.

The industrial revolution slowly gathered momentum, and England began the painful process of becoming the first country to convert itself willingly from a labour-intensive agricultural nation to an urban state in which factories and mills belching smoke and soot threatened to disfigure the landscape. When William Blake wrote of 'England's green and pleasant land' and 'Dark satanic mills', in the same prophetic poem he was warning everyone of the dangers inherent in a change he judged to be for the worse. William Wordsworth, Keats, Shelley, all wrote of a pastoral country in danger of despoilation and although their worst fears have not been realised—in the late twentieth-century England is *still* a Green and Pleasant Land—their doubts and uncertainties were fully justified by what they witnessed at the time.

George Stephenson and his railways did as much as anyone to make industrial change possible; so did Robert Macadam, in using broken stones set in tar, to make smooth roads possible; Thomas Telford built bridges and huge commercial warehouses; Thomas Cubitt used his creative genius and an eye for quick profit to build elegant town houses and a number of deep-water docks for ships. Steam-engines powered by coal were the motive force that made it all possible, and whilst it might be comforting to imagine that parliamentary government was fully in control of events that were reshaping England, they were not. Private enterprise and men greedy for huge profits were the instigators of Britain's development as the world's first industrial nation, transforming the raw materials of empire into goods that could be sold overseas for handsome rewards. As a nation Great Britain was rich and powerful and this gave her the strength to impose a semblance of peace world-wide and to arbitrate in other countries' disputes. At the same time territory overseas was colonised, bringing civilisation to the native inhabitants, whether they wanted it or not. On the whole, Britain's empire-building was mutually beneficial: diseases were first checked and then conquered; Christianity was spread with a missionary zeal; and British engineers built roads, railways and bridges in a network of communications that have stood the test of time. Many countries now enjoying their independence have cause to be grateful for the irrigation and fresh-water projects supplied by Britain more than a hundred years ago.

Meanwhile, what of King George the Third, thought to be a lunatic in 1790 and shunted away to Windsor Castle where he made little impact on public affairs?

In rare moments of lucidity he signed state documents, saw ministers and remained just on the brink of being regarded as incapable of continuing as king. However, during the winter of 1810-11 Prime Minister Spencer Perceval (the only British premier to be assassinated, in 1812, although from purely private and non-political motives) proposed that the king's eldest son, George, should be appointed Prince Regent to take over all royal duties and, on 5th February 1811, Prince George became king in all but name.

The Prince Regent had always been wayward and wilful as heir to the throne but now his extravagances became positively reckless. He spent lavishly on new buildings, encouraging the architect, John Nash, to change the face of London as no other king had done before or since. Regent's Park and Regent Street, Carlton House, Buckingham Palace and the Theatre Royal Haymarket all owe their existence to Prince George. He also built the exuberant fantasy of an oriental palace known as the Brighton Pavilion so that he could enjoy the seaside delights of Brighton with Maria Fitzherbert, whom he had secretly and illegally married in 1785. Prince George was an art connoisseur of the very highest degree; he supported the foundation of London's National Gallery and it was the gift of his own collection of 70,000 books that began the British Museum although the building was not completed until after his death.

Notwithstanding his illegal marriage to the Catholic Mrs Fitzherbert he was obliged, as a royal duty, to marry a German princess and so produce children to continue the royal line of succession. In the event, his marriage to Princess Caroline of Brunswick proved an utter disaster and Prince George never ceased to hate and detest her from the moment they first met. They lived together for only a short time and their only child, Charlotte, was destined to become England's first queen since the death of Queen Anne in 1714. Unfortunately her destiny was unfulfilled because she died in 1818 and threw the royal line of succession into confusion. Prince George had a total of eight brothers and six sisters, and the elder brothers now raced to find suitable brides for themselves and produce children, so that whoever succeeded to the throne would have no shortage of heirs.

Only dimly aware of the undignified behaviour of his sons King George the Third declined into a senility from which death released him on 29th January 1820 at the age of 81. He had been king for almost sixty years, a length of time only to be exceeded by his granddaughter, Victoria.

The Prince Regent, now King George the Fourth, was no longer young himself and through illness could not attend his father's burial at Windsor but he recovered in time to enjoy one of the most lavish coronations ever recorded. After a five hour service in Westminster Abbey, he joined three hundred male guests at a banquet in Westminster Hall followed by a firework display in Hyde park. The only sour note on such a spectacular day was when Queen Caroline was refused admittance to her husband's coronation service. Earlier the new king had tried to annul his unfortunate marriage on the grounds of the queen's alleged adultery with an obscure Italian, Bartolemo Pergami, and she was obliged to undergo a trial by Parliament. The 'trial' was a fiasco from start to finish and ended ingloriously when Parliament abandoned their proceedings due to lack of evidence. In truth, Queen Caroline was very popular and it has been claimed that demonstrations supporting her diverted the public's attention away from the political unrest beginning to surface as Parliament continued to hesitate over reforming itself.

King George the Fourth as a prince had been partisan in supporting some political friends at the expense of others but as king he became merely pompous and fully aware of his power of patronage and prerogative. This showed itself in 1822 when Viscount Castlereagh, architect of England's foreign policy since the Congress of Vienna, cut his throat with a penknife and bled himself to death. He had led the House of Commons with some distinction, even though Lord Russell, sitting in the House of Lords, was Prime Minister. George Canning, a friend of Queen Caroline, was Parliament's choice to succeed Castlereagh and King George tried every expedient to thwart Canning's appointment. The Duke of Wellington, politically ambitious, supported the king even though he was Canning's political colleague. King George's interference in diplomatic activities caused much confusion abroad and only when the king could no longer afford to ignore Canning's great popularity did he relent, even to the extent of accepting Canning as a loyal friend. Indeed, he was appointed Prime Minister to follow Lord Russell but died less than six months later. The king also objected to the Catholic Emancipation Bill which allowed Catholics to hold public office again, and only at the very end of his life did King George agree to give his approval to Parliament's wishes.

Acting out a monarchial role suited King George the Fourth

very well. As Prince Regent, he appeared to take personal responsibility for Wellington's success at Waterloo and as king he indulged himself to the full in the wearing of uniforms decorated by medals and awards. He deserves to be remembered for his great patronage of all the arts—especially painting and sculpture—and when he died on 26th June 1830 in Windsor, much of the glamour of ceremonial kingship died with him.

His brother, Prince William, who now succeeded had made the Royal Navy his career and he is still known as 'the sailor king'. It was because of his height in the confined spaces below deck that led to his royal command that on board naval ships the loyal toast should be drank seated; a tradition still maintained today. As a young man he lived for many years with a married woman, an actress called Mrs Jordans, and together they produced ten illegitimate children. With the prospect of kingship looming after the death of Princess Charlotte in 1818, Prince William married a German princess, Adelaide, after whom the Australian city is named.

King William the Fourth and Queen Adelaide were no longer young and could have no hope of further children after their two daughters died in infancy. Nevertheless the king was popular and he did take his duties seriously.

He presided over the Reform Bill of 1832 and gave the Act his firm support, threatening to swamp the House of Lords with friends sympathetic to his wishes if the peers, led by a stubborn and reactionary Duke of Wellington, obstructed the reform of Parliament. King William was very much aware of social conditions within his kingdom and it might be argued that his seven year reign was dull, uneventful and free from that corruption and scandal which so excites the public taste for high drama. At the same time republicanism declined as a political issue and agitation for political change seemed to have been pacified by a Parliament bent on self-reform.

Compared to the extravagances and over-ripe personality of his brother George, King William brought stability and a sense of decorum to the royal family and these gave his niece Victoria a foundation on which to build.

12

VICTORIA (1837 to 1901)

Just before dawn, on 20th June 1837, Princess Victoria was summoned from her bed in Kensington Palace and greeted by the Archbishop of Canterbury, the Prime Minister Lord Melbourne (who, like Queen Adelaide, gave his name to an Australian city) and other dignitaries of the establishment. In a touching little ceremony, these grand gentlemen knelt at the feet of an eighteen-year old girl to tell her that Uncle William, King William the Fourth, had died and that she was now Queen of England.

The girl's father had been Duke of Kent, fourth son of George the Third, and one of the brothers who had rushed into marriage when Princess Charlotte had died in 1818. A year later his only child, Victoria, was born and in the following year he himself died leaving a widow, a pile of debts, and a daughter who was likely to be Queen of England one day. The Duchess of Kent was a formidable lady of aristocratic German origins and she brought up her daughter in a manner some observers thought to be too rigid and protective, even to the extent of sleeping every night in Princess Victoria's bedroom. On her very first day as queen, Victoria broke free in dramatic fashion; she began by excluding her mother from the first Council Meeting and ended by ordering the duchess's bed placed in a separate room so that Queen Victoria enjoyed total privacy for the first time on the very day she ascended the throne. This spirit of independence, staunch, forthright and courageous, would be a characteristic of her long and eventful reign.

Almost at once she abandoned her childhood home, Kensington Palace, and moved to the newly-completed Buckingham Palace with its grand ballrooms and large elegant areas, especially designed for lavish entertainments. Victoria was the first sovereign to use Buckingham Palace and she lost no time in arranging dances and parties for guests by the hundred. After so many years of a moribund court dominated by elderly kings, this new round of lively gaiety was welcomed by London's fashionable society. Victoria clearly enjoyed the pleasure of being an eighteen-year old queen, dining and dancing at night, learning to be a constitutional monarch by day.

Queen Victoria radiated patriotism from head to toe and always responded to her duties as sovereign, even though she never lost the dangerous habit of favouring some ministers at the expense of others. She adored her first Prime Minister, Lord Melbourne, and was quick to learn from him the nature of her responsibilities. One of these was, quite clearly, to find a suitable husband.

The English royal family had so many connections with the royal households of German states that it caused no surprise when Prince Albert of Saxe-Coburg-Gotha, who had visited England previously to meet his cousin Princess Victoria, was invited to return as a prospective husband for the young queen and, in February 1840, he and Victoria were married in the chapel of St. James's Palace. Queen Victoria at the age of twenty-one was no prude and she loved Albert as passionately and physically as any woman could love any man. Together they produced nine children, who between them wed into the royal families of Sweden, Norway, Spain, Romania, Russia, Denmark and the newly-unified state of Germany. Little wonder that long before her death, Queen Victoria was known as the 'Grandmother of Europe'.

Prince Albert returned Victoria's affection in full measure whilst at the same time appearing stiff, formal and polite to those outside his intimate circle. He was an intellectual with a sound knowledge of science and physics. He could paint, write verse, compose music, and so give patronage to the arts that was based on well-informed personal experience. Mendelssohn's success and popularity owes much to royal patronage, as did the group of talented painters known collectively as the Pre-Raphaelite Brothers, because they based their technique and subject matter on that of the Italian Renaissance in general and Raphael in particular; that fifteenth century artist being Prince Albert's especial favourite. The prince was also responsible for introducing the Christmas Tree to England from his native Germany and many of our traditional yule-tide festivities owe their origins to Prince Albert. Victoria also gained from Albert not merely culture but a sense of high moral purpose that underlined her own strong sense of duty.

From the early days of her political tutelage under Lord Melbourne, Queen Victoria took a keen and lively interest both in party politics and in the day-to-day running of individual government departments. Albert shared his wife's interest in affairs of state but found it difficult to accept Queen Victoria's role as a constitutional and not an absolute monarch. In an attempt to mitigate Albert's frustration, the queen offered him some degree of official recognition by according him the title, dignity and authority of Prince Consort. It made little difference. Albert was denied the responsibility he craved for, by a democratically elected government that was quite capable of organising itself without the assistance of either a young inexperienced queen or her German-born husband.

Sir Robert Peel, who had displaced Victoria's beloved Lord Melbourne, was an early recipient of royal disfavour, although the queen reserved her greatest displeasure for Lord Palmerston, the foreign minister. His critics—and Queen Victoria was one—thought him arrogant, rude and prone to give too much encouragement to the revolutionary groups in continental Europe, who were agitating for social change. His numerous supporters both inside and outside Parliament approved of his desire to export the principle of England's constitutional monarchy into some of Europe's despotic kingdoms. Palmerston was nevertheless impatient with minor revolts in territories which had British interests; his solution to all such problems was to despatch a small military force to restore order with ruthless efficiency and his routine instruction to 'send a gunboat' gave rise to the phrase still used to describe such policy as 'gunboat diplomacy'. Victoria herself was the frequent victim of Palmerston's disdainful attitude towards kings and princes who disagreed with him, and their quarrels about the conduct of foreign affairs threatened to become constitutionally serious. Undoubtedly he resented the private visits—which often assumed the importance of State Occasions—made by Victoria and Albert to their royal relations on continental Europe: a Europe rapidly becoming a revolutionary cauldron which in 1848 boiled over.

Italy, Austria, Denmark, Germany and France were all affected by the revolutionary spirit that swept across Europe, overthrowing governments and monarchies with its demands for change and social reform. Queen Victoria held Palmerston personally responsible for causing King Louis Philippe and his French royal family to seek sanctuary in England as Napoleon Bonaparte's nephew was declared President of the new French republic. For once Palmerston had gone too far and was obliged to resign although he would later surface as Prime Minister to serve his queen and country with loyalty and sound administrative skill.

In spite of the discontent surging across continental Europe England escaped with only small-scale demonstrations, and these from a group calling themselves Chartists, who argued that the 1832 Reform Bill had not been drastic enough, but even these modest intentions failed to command widespread popular support.

Charles Dickens painted a picture of Victorian England that was bleak and apparently ripe for violent change, and yet it never happened. The poor; the homeless; the unemployed; the sick; and the unfortunate members of the community who were plagued by all these miseries deserved a compassion that was slow in arriving. By creating a host of unforgettable characters and placing them in the setting of dirty and overcrowded cities, Charles Dickens used his narrative genius to focus attention on what was happening to whole sections of an impoverished society. And yet the image of nineteenth century England created by Dickens was not the whole picture.

In contrast to the stark wretchedness of life's unfortunate victims, many members of the aristocracy, the land-owning gentlemen and the wealthy industrial magnates, wallowed in unashamed luxury, their country estates and opulent London mansions becoming focal points for the idle rich who were growing richer week by week. Nevertheless some of society's upper echelon were developing a guilty conscience and they began taking steps which would lead to further Reform Bills in 1859 and 1866; together, these reforms added most of the working classes to the electoral register. The oppressive Corn Law—in effect a tax on food—was abolished, bringing with it cheaper bread and flour. Gradually, a mood of optimism began to pervade, that, given time and patience, life for those at a disadvantage would get better. The English spirit of 'evolution not revolution' might not have been understood in France or Austria but in the cities and countryside of Great Britain it certainly was; due mainly to the rapidly increasing influence of a newly emergent class of society.

Between the self-indulgent rich and the under-privileged poor, both groups representing only a minority, there appeared a strong middle-class that was industrious, full of enterprise, eager for self-improvement and with resolute moral principles. It was their vitality and natural obedience which made Britain's industrial revolution into a rip-roaring success. They provided the engineers to build roads and railways, design bridges and tunnels, and the teachers to educate the masses. Factories began to provide not merely cheaply-produced goods but items of real quality from steam locomotives and machine tools to well-designed cutlery and furniture.

A natural consequence of this wealth-creating industry was the Great Exhibition of 1851. Many individuals claimed the credit for thinking of an exhibition at which the world would come to London and see the rich fruits of England's enterprise and industry, although Prince Albert was the man who organised what we now recognise as the world's first 'Trade Fair'. A site in Hyde Park was chosen, a huge glass pavilion—called The Crystal Palace—was designed and built by Joseph Paxton as the centre-piece. Under Queen Victoria's patronage and Prince Albert's direction, the Great Exhibition combined the native splendour and raw material of Britain's empire with the resources and strength that had created a mighty industrial revolution. Throughout the summer of 1851 the world came to London to marvel at England's inventiveness and, much more important, to place orders.

The country's unashamed pride in its achievements was reflected in a growing appreciation of the Royal Family. It was as if the people now realised they had a monarchy to be proud of, a Parliament that was slowly coming to reflect popular opinion, and that they had become part of the most powerful nation on earth.

A measure of this power was that in 1854 Britain could afford to fight an all-out war against Russia and take it in her stride. Liberal sentiment demanded that England should support Turkey in that country's quarrel with Russia; especially as defeat for Turkey would give Russia an outlet from the Black Sea into the wealth and riches of the Mediterranean. The conflict is known as the Crimean War. It revealed the shameful way weapons, tactics and training in the British Army had been neglected since Wellington's day. (The Iron Duke, incidentally, had died in 1852, his anti-working class reactionary views now forgotten and forgiven as he was given a hero's funeral in St Paul's Cathedral, as lavish and spectacular an occasion as that accorded to Nelson.) Two events are remembered from the Crimean War; The Charge of the Light Brigade and Florence Nightingale's caring for wounded soldiers whilst holding aloft her famous lamp.

Due to muddle, ineptitude and the sort of downright carelessness which was a hallmark of the Crimean campaign, a whole regiment of lightly armed cavalry were ordered to attack a well-defended battery of Russian artillery near Sebastapol. Lord Cardigan led the charge into the enemy guns but only at appalling cost in British lives were the cannons silenced. One of the captured Russian guns was brought to London and the metal used to provide the bronze medal which is Britain's highest award for courage in the face of the enemy: the Victoria Cross, or V.C., is simply engraved 'For Valour'. Florence Nightingale's work of tending the wounded in conditions that were squalid and primitive was both heroic and of lasting consequence. Because of her tenacity, the army medical services were reorganised from top to bottom and after the war she founded a school in London to train nurses and give them professional status, a sense of duty, and the skill in caring for patients they have never lost.

The Crimean War ended in defeat for the Russians and

effectively halted their ambition of vaulting over Turkey and entering Europe 'through the unprotected back door'. As that war ended another conflict began—this time in India where the native army, supervised by the British, mutinied and for a time threatened the stability of that teeming sub-continent. The British government decided that the East India Company, founded during the reign of Elizabeth the First, had outlived its usefulness as a purely commercial enterprise and it was decided to impose direct rule from Parliament at Westminster. Queen Victoria was declared the sovereign over India and in due course Parliament would confer the title Empress of India upon her.

Such considerations were abruptly made to seem unimportant to Queen Victoria because, on 14th December 1861, Prince Albert died of typhoid, a victim of the poor sanitation and unhygienic conditions within Windsor Castle. Queen Victoria was grief-stricken, a widow at 42 with forty more years to live. Albert left a void in her life no-one else could fill and she mourned, publicly and privately, until the day she died. One man who did more than anyone to help the queen overcome her deeply felt grief was the Conservative politician Benjamin Disreali, a Jew who was both intensely patriotic and devoted to his queen.

He was witty, charming, and had the ability and appetite to flatter and cajole Queen Victoria as only Lord Melbourne had done before. Given time he would have persuaded the queen to appear in public again much earlier than she did, but after only a few months as Prime Minister the Conservatives lost control and William Ewart Gladstone, the Liberal (as the Whigs were now known), began the first of his four spells as Queen Victoria's chief minister. He adopted a high moral line on every issue and could be pompous, self-righteous and an insufferable bore to those unappreciative of his liberal instincts. The queen loathed him and was once heard to complain: 'He speaks to me as if he is addressing a public meeting!'. For six years she endured Gladstone and listened impatiently to his views on giving self-rule to Ireland. Then he, in turn, was rejected by the electorate and to the queen's undisguised joy, Benjamin Disreali returned.

Disreali's reputation as a novelist of some distinction was by this time well-known, (so too was that of another contemporary politician, Anthony Trollope who served as Postmaster General, a position which gave him an insight into the political manoeuvering he depicted so authentically in his books), and his relationship with Queen Victoria was that of a sympathetic friend rather than Prime Minister. Although, as leader of the Conservative party, he was dedicated to maintaining institutions as they were, rather than reforming them, he was aware of the widening gulf between rich and poor and he coined the phrase 'two nations' to emphasise how wide that gulf had become. In spite of promoting the Public Health Act of 1875 and the Artisan Housing Act, he was forced to accept that the gap between ordinary people and the privileged was too wide to be bridged by small-scale legislation. Neither was Disreali enthusiastic about the British Empire, which he thought was a handicap rather than an asset. Instead his foreign interests were concerned with Europe and ensuring Russia was kept at arms length. Nevertheless, Disreali was both a patriot and an opportunist and by an astute action he seized a chance of buying a major shareholding in the newly-opened Suez Canal on behalf of England and told Parliament only when the deal was completed.

Like a wealthy brother indulging his favourite sister Disreali used his powers of persuasion within Parliament to bestow the title Empress of India upon Queen Victoria, a distinction that delighted the queen. She revealed her pleasure by surrounding herself with Indian *objets d'art* and allowing a number of Indian natives to serve as her loyal attendants; she also made Disreali a peer and he took the title of Earl of Beaconsfield.

Slowly, Queen Victoria emerged from the shadow of Albert's death and fitfully assumed the public duties as Queen and Empress. She was greatly encouraged at the popular acclaim she received and even though seldom appearing dressed in any colour other than black, she was invariably dignified with a regal authority that seemed to stamp her personality upon the nation and her reign.

The Victorian Age of the late nineteenth century had reached a zenith in English History that would never be surpassed or equalled.

Overseas, the empire was both stable and continuing to

expand. Early fears that Canada might seek independence had evaporated and both the major territories of Australia and New Zealand regarded themselves as British as any corner of Oxford, Westminster or Stratford upon Avon. India, whilst retaining the identity and culture of its own country, was now under direct British rule and becoming influenced by English traditions. A whole host of Pacific and Oriental territories were ruled beneath the British flag without much conflict of interest and only in Africa was there resistance to British Imperialism. Much of Africa south of the Nile delta remained unexplored by European traders until men like David Livingstone ventured where few white men had been before. In what is now South Africa there was friction between the British settlers and those of mainly Dutch extraction (Afrikaaners or Boers) and further to the north some tribes of brave native warriors like the Zulus and Ashanti fought a stubborn rearguard battle to delay British annexation of their territory.

Further north still, in the Nile valley, Britain extended her influence even more. For many years, Egypt was considered part of the Turkish Ottoman Empire, but this empire was disintegrating and leaving a vacuum in an area vital to British commercial interests; not least of which was the Suez Canal. A complication was that the Upper Nile had resisted British Imperialism, with the tribe of Sudanese slave-traders, led by a religious fanatic called the Mahdi, resenting British involvement in their country. In 1885 William Ewart Gladstone, back as Prime Minister again, decided to evacuate Sudan until Egypt was fully under British control and he selected a national hero, General Gordon, to lead an expedition to Khartoum and organise the withdrawal. General Gordon chose to stay and fight, although his stubborness in the face of overwhelming odds cost him his own life and those of the Khartoum garrison. The event was seen as a national catastrophe, Queen Victoria was furious, and Gladstone was lucky to ride out the storm and win the next general election.

At home, Queen Victoria's long reign had seen wealth and prosperity flow into the nation's coffers, even though not every individual appeared to have shared their country's good fortune.

Many of the institutions accepted and admired today were

created during this period, and the efficiency of local government in large towns and cities served as models for other countries to follow. Municipal authorities built their town halls with an architectural style that reflected their grandeur and power. Piped water that was safe and pure began to be available in every home, so was gas for lighting and cooking, the same gas that now illuminated well-maintained streets. Horse-drawn buses and trams charging low fares were a familiar sight and by 1863 London had built the world's first underground railway.

New schools to provide accommodation for a growing number of schoolchildren had to be erected, giving effect to the 1870 Education Act. This Act made it compulsory for boys and girls to attend school until attaining the age of twelve, such schools to be supported from public funds and no longer relying on the charity of voluntary organisations. Municipal authorities found it less easy to sweep away all the cheaply-built dwellings that had satisfied the demands of a population abandoning agriculture in favour of all the uncertainties of city life. A century of non-existent town-planning had left a legacy of slum houses unfit for human habitation, a breeding ground for petty crime, drunkenness and an infant mortality rate that was no less shocking for becoming commonplace. It would take another two generations for these Dickensian houses to be destroyed and replaced.

Even so, it was a sign of increased prosperity for many, with leisure time in which to spend it, that games such as football and cricket became spectator sports for the first time. Music Halls proliferated in every district, playing popular variety acts to capacity audiences, whilst at the same time Gilbert and Sullivan set new standards with their comic operas at London's Savoy Theatre, where for the first time, electric lights replaced gas in a public building. Progress to benefit everyone seemed everywhere. By now the Royal Mail postal service had become well-established and taken for granted. Letters collected from red boxes now to be seen on almost every street corner were delivered to any house or cottage in the country for a flat rate of only one penny (pre-1970 decimal coinage) and this was paid by licking a black stamp, bearing Queen Victoria's head, on the envelope and these early 'penny blacks' have become one of the rarest of all postage stamps.

Other institutions were born in circumstances that shamed the period of Victoria's reign. So many children were orphaned or abandoned to fend for themselves that a certain Doctor Barnardo began a charity specifically to care for them; it continues as a charitable organisation to perform the same function today. William Booth was another man concerned with the drunkenness and foolish gambling of working men and he resolved to save their souls and their bodies by founding the Salvation Army; it, too, continues to fulfill a useful role with great success and much popular and sympathetic support. Other voluntary agencies and philanthropic groups, too numerous to mention, established themselves to alleviate the suffering of men, women and children who had fallen on hard times, some of them enduring vile conditions inside overcrowded prisons or 'houses of correction'. Penal reform had taken place during the century; the punishment of 'transportation' (being exiled to one of the colonies and forced to work there in conditions worse than many English prisons) had stopped in 1846. Twenty-two years later, public executions, perhaps the most degrading of all nineteenth century exper- iences, also ceased, although the number of capital offences still on the statute book kept several public-hangmen gainfully em- ployed behind closed doors. Long periods of imprisonment for non-payment of debts or minor offences would continue into the reign of Edward the Seventh.

Governments of both political parties were reluctant to abandon their policy of *laisez faire*, non-interference in affairs that did not directly concern the state. This notion of self-help and mutual assistance between one man and his neighbour has come to be regarded as the creed of 'Victorian values', which we either admire or decry according to an individual's political point of view. What cannot be denied is that the Victorian period marked the high tide of the 'family' as a close-knit unit, and of church attendance as a Sunday routine.

The father had become the undisputed head of a Victorian family and the views of his children and their mother became totally subservient to his. Many families owned pianos both as a status symbol and as a means of entertainment; an evening gathered round the piano singing sentimental ballads was a regular feature of life in Victorian England. So was bible-reading and saying grace before meals a standard extending into almost every home whether in the upper, middle or working class.

Religion had ceased to be a destructive element in society but it continued to be divisive to some extent. The upper classes invariably attended the Church of England, usually referred to as 'Church', whilst the middle and lower classes went to one of the 'free churches' such as Methodist, Baptist or Weslyan; usually referred to as 'Chapel'. Coincidental with England's Industrial Revolution had come an evangelical movement spearheaded by John and Samuel Wesley, men who despised bishops and all the rich trappings of what they regarded as ritual. Their free-thinking ideas appealed to the working classes particularly and chapels devoid of formal altars were to be seen as frequently as the gothic spires and towers of the established Church of England.

If religion had ceased to be a matter for political debate, the fate of Ireland was still a subject of fierce controversy. Gladstone staked his reputation on giving Ireland some measure of self-determination, only to find to his cost that his ideas were not popular. Generations of Englishmen had regarded Ireland as a thorn in their side, although regarding its removal as more painful than leaving it there. They were aware that a great part of Ireland, the south, had remained Catholic when Henry the Eighth had engineered his Reformation in 1536, and aware that the Irish had felt themselves alien to the English long before that. The problem was that others in Ireland, Protestants in the northern part, Ulster, did not relish losing their traditional ties with Britain and its monarchy. Gladstone tried hard to resolve this dilemma by offering a measure of home-rule to Ireland whilst protecting the legitimate interests of loyal citizens in Ulster. However he could no more square the circle than any other politician before or since. It was this issue which defeated Gladstone in 1886 and led to a long period of strong Conservative government under Lord Salisbury, a descendant of Elizabeth the First's great Chancellor. Disreali had died in 1881 and Gladstone followed in 1898, two political giants who had opposed each other for almost half a century, yet who had rendered service to their queen and country in their different ways.

Queen Victoria sailed into the last two decades of her life like a stately galleon; dignified, respected, and almost invulnerable. Her prestige among the despotic crowned heads of Europe to which she was related proved itself to be of great diplomatic advantage, and her status as the regal distant figure of 'the Great White Queen across the sea' was a unifying element within the British Empire at a time when Parliament and government were indifferent to the concept of an empire for its own sake. With the premature death of Prince Albert she lost the man who might have stimulated her intellectually. As it was, her tastes in music, art and fashion became commonplace and it was widely believed and accepted that although she had the awesome presence of majesty she could, if given the opportunity, be equally at home in a small country cottage. She had a stubborn nature and an innate experience of what was right for her people both in England and her empire.

In 1887 she celebrated the Golden Jubilee of being Queen for fifty years and a thousand statues bearing her likeness appeared in many a public square or municipal park, reflecting the esteem and popularity in which she was held. This widespread feeling of universal affection pleased Victoria very much, and she now braced herself for the even greater achievement of 1897 when she would enjoy her Diamond Jubilee of a sixty-year reign.

One event blighted that 1897 jubilee: the war in South Africa, known as the Boer War, coincided with the queen's celebration. For several years there had been friction between the British colony at the tip of southern Africa, Cape Colony centred around Capetown, and the largely Dutch-speaking settlers further north. They were called Afrikaaners or Boers (Boer or Boor being Dutch for farmer) and further north still was the ill-defined area being colonised under the British flag by Cecil Rhodes, a tactless undiplomatic opportunist, who nevertheless created the modern state of Rhodesia, now Zimbabwe. With an eye on the lucrative gold-fields and diamond mines, Rhodes and his friends made incursions into Boer territory and it was such a raid led by Leander Jameson (The Jameson Raid) which provoked the Boers and dragged, almost unwillingly, Britain and the Boers into an all-out war.

At first Britain did not take the Boers seriously and a number of British garrisons were surrounded; the town of Mafeking was beseiged for 215 days before relief came and the Relief of Mafeking was celebrated in England with so much rejoicing that the event assumed the importance of a great national victory. The seige greatly enhanced the reputation of Mafeking's military commander, Colonel Robert Baden-Powell, who drew on the experience when he started the Boy Scout movement. Slowly, Britain mobilised her military strength and decisively crushed the Boers to unify the whole of South Africa under the British flag. To all intents the Boer War ended in 1900 but for a further two years the Dutch farmers waged an unofficial guerrilla war that embarrassed the British government, and the military leaders had great difficulty in searching for the small number of Boers who evaded capture and attacked British settlements until 1902.

Queen Victoria came to be seen as the very embodiment of the nineteenth century, and not merely in England or the British Empire. Victorian is accepted shorthand to describe the period, even by nations completely independent of Britain. For sixty years Victoria had presided over a country that had progressed from an agricultural and rural society into a modern industrial state, evolving and reforming its parliamentary institutions by degrees rather than dramatic upsets in the balance of power. No other comparable country has done this without revolution or civil war.

When Queen Victoria died peacefully at Osborne House—appropriately the house designed by Prince Albert—on 22nd January 1901 at the age of 81, she had reigned for sixty-three years, seven months and two days; the longest reign of any English sovereign before or since. Her lavish state funeral was attended by kings, queens and emperors from many nations and the event was seen even then as a watershed, the end of an era, and many people were heard to whisper: 'England will never be the same without The Old Queen'. Their prophesy was not slow to be fulfilled.

13

The death of Queen Victoria coincided with a feeling that Great Britain's role as a truly independent power was about to end.

For over one hundred years the country had enjoyed the luxury of unbridled freedom of action in almost every part of the world. From Palmerston's 'gunboat diplomacy' to Lord Salisbury's decision to 'teach the Boers a lesson', Britain had used its muscle-power of industrial strength to maintain a large Royal Navy which, allied to a modest professional army, had been sufficient to protect British interests and trade routes the world over. This cosy isolationism was about to end, and the man responsible was one of the chief mourners who, proud and erect, walked behind the gun-carriage bearing Queen Victoria's coffin.

Kaiser Wilhelm II, autocratic ruler of the new imperial state of Germany, was the son of Queen Victoria's eldest daughter, who shared her mother's name but was more usually known as Vicky. The Kaiser had shown a devotion to his grandmother amounting to reverence and he insisted on being present when the old queen died; only protocol prevented him taking personal charge of the funeral arrangements. He greatly respected and admired English virtues and traditions, to such an extent that he positively hero-worshipped the memory of Admiral Nelson. Unfortunately, Kaiser Wilhelm had few diplomatic skills, and he made no friends in England when he voiced support for the Boers in their fight against the British army. He was equally tactless in offending Queen Victoria's eldest son, on more than one occasion forgetting that the Prince of Wales—the Kaiser's uncle—would reign as King Edward the Seventh.

Diplomatic and social niceties apart, a more sinister element had entered the relationship between Great Britain and the Kaiser. His admiration for the Royal Navy had made him envious and he now began an expansion of his own navy that could hardly be justified by Germany's short coastline and insignificant colonial territories in Africa. Already the Kaiser's army, steeped in Prussian militarism which gave army officers an enviable place in German high-society, was the most powerful on continental Europe. It had proved itself in 1870 by defeating France almost without effort. To guard itself against such a reoccurence, France had formed an alliance with Russia and at the time of Queen Victoria's death Kaiser Wilhelm nursed ambitions to ally his all-conquering army with Britain's powerful Royal Navy. Instead, Great Britain safeguarded her interests in the Far East by forming an alliance with Japan, whose navy had recently defeated a numerically superior Russian fleet in a war that revealed Russia's inadequacies. Meanwhile, in Europe, the pressures and challenges from Germany were politely resisted by a British government aware that many countries were developing their own industrial bases and forming alliances of self-protection with each other. Weapons of war, and strategic planning to mobilise them, had become far more sophisticated and, almost unwillingly, countries began to enlarge and modernise their armed forces.

One important factor in all this was the character and personal preferences of England's new king, Edward the Seventh. Sixty years old at his accession he did not share the pro-German sympathies of his parents and Hanoverian ancestors, and the earlier offensive behaviour of his nephew, Kaiser Wilhelm, had done nothing to alter this. King Edward had always taken his pleasures seriously: gambling at cards, owning race-horses and attending race-meetings, eating rich food in gargantuan quantities not seen in royal circles since the days of Henry the Eighth, and drinking fine wine, champagne especially. As well as being happily married to Alexandra, a royal Danish princess who remained beautiful all her life, the king enjoyed the company of attractively witty ladies; the actress Lillie Langtry was to be a great favourite, so was Mrs Alice Keppel. King Edward was also keenly interested in the world of diplomacy and even before his mother's death he came to realise that it would be in Europe, not the British Empire, where England's fate must be decided.

If Queen Victoria could be regarded as the Grandmother of Europe then King Edward was undoubtedly the Uncle of Europe. In addition to Kaiser Wilhelm another great ruler was his nephew, Tsar Nicholas of Russia, and very few other royal houses did not have some sort of blood relationship with England's king, of much importance in an age when quarrels or friendships within the 'European royal family' could have serious diplomatic repercussions. The opposite was also true, a popular regard for a foreign king often eased difficulties between governments and the relationship between King Edward and the people of France is a good illustration how important royal influence still was. For almost a century an armed truce had existed between the two countries and if war was never a serious danger then it was also true that there was little sincere friendship either. King Edward changed all that.

He had visited France privately—sometimes using a fictitious name to avoid publicity—and enjoyed all the pleasures that Paris in the late nineteenth-century could offer. Only here could he consort as he wished with intelligent witty women, and be entertained in a society where attractive ladies presided at *soirées* and in their famous *salons*; in London the clubs were orientated around male society and this held few attractions for King Edward. An alliance with France seemed to the king much more natural and desirable than one with Germany; always provided the general public of both countries would give such an agreement their popular support.

In 1904 King Edward the Seventh decided to test the atmosphere, and at a personal risk of being jeered at in public, or rebuffed by Parisians who might be hostile, he made a State Visit to France and agreed to ride down the boulevards of Paris in an open carriage. At first the French were not too welcoming, but under the charismatic warmth of King Edward's personality the crowds began to cheer him and the visit turned into a royal triumph. It was perhaps the greatest service Edward the Seventh could have rendered his country, and one for which France would be equally grateful. The governments of both countries seized the opportunity and signed the famous *Entente Cordiale* which was not a full-blooded cast-iron treaty but it was enough to bind both countries closer together, tacitly acknowledging the rising power of Germany as their main potental enemy.

During the next ten years there were a number of diplomatic incidents underlining the instability that had arisen in Europe since Germany became one united country instead of fragmented princeling states. On the one hand Germany and the vast ramshackle Austro-Hungarian Empire were in triple alliance with Italy, surrounded by an alliance of France, Russia and England, with Belgium trying to remain neutral but aware that Germany might one day cross her borders to strike an early blow at France. These loosely-knit alliances resembled armed camps in which generals and admirals plotted to perfect their plans and train their forces; to the world at large there was little anxiety and no hostility between the people of one country with another. Kings and princes travelled freely within each other's countries as an air of peace and contentment settled like a gentle zephyr over central and western Europe: in Russia and the Balkans a seething dissatisfaction bubbled into sporadic violence, as peasants and ill-paid factory workers tried to improve their conditions by changing the system that governed them, events that were of little concern to anyone else in the rest of Europe.

For the rich and privileged, England during the reign of Edward the Seventh must have seemed like one long garden-party under royal patronage. Wealthy industrialists, although unable to buy themselves titles and honours directly, donated a proportion of their money to charity or supported worthwhile causes, and were rewarded by the occasional knighthood, viscountcy or even earldom. Many numbered the king or his lady-friends among their circle of weekend guests, and to them the world must have seemed an untroubled place. The king openly enjoyed the pageantry and splendour of military parades; the pomp and circumstance of a powerful country that was proud of its military glory. During summer afternoons almost every park in London and the large cities featured an army band entertaining the populance who put on their best clothes to take their exercise, especially on Sunday after morning church or chapel.

An autumnal glow, inspired by King Edward's zest for life and the country's self-evident prosperity, spread across England. The spirit and mood of this period can be recaptured by listening to the music of Edward Elgar: all the pageantry and opulence is there, all the natural beauty of a landscape miraculously spared from industrial spoilation, all the radiance of people happy and free from internal strife. And yet there is a sadness in the music too, a wistful nostalgia that can still make a sensitive listener hold his or her breath. The Edwardian glow was a twilight reflection from the Victorian way of life now inevitably doomed, and whether Edward Elgar knew this or not is irrelevant: it is mirrored in his music.

Parliamentary politics were shifting their ground too, not dramatically but with that degree of significant evolution that has made English democracy unique.

England has always made a home for radicals, dissatisfied malcontents who refused to believe that the poor and helpless should be denied justice and a greater share in their country's wealth. King John's reluctant agreement to Magna Carta in 1215 began it all, later came the creation of Parliament in 1265, the Peasant's Revolt of 1381 and Jack Cade's Rebellion of 1450 each made their point before being crushed; Oliver Cromwell was more successful in leading Parliament to victory over King Charles the First but the Industrial Revolution led to discontent of a different nature, when poorly-paid workers tried to join together in 'trade-unions' and these groupings were banned by a succession of governments who could see the dangers of such concerted action. In 1834 at the Dorset town of Tolpuddle six men suffered the punishment of transportation for illegally swearing an oath of loyalty to their trade union. Now remembered as the Tolpuddle Martyrs their sacrifice led to the legality of Trade Unions and during the reign of King Edward the Seventh such unions became not merely legal but positively sanctified and placed above the law.

Throughout the reigns of William the Fourth, Queen Victoria and now Edward the Seventh a number of reform bills had been enacted by Parliament, more and more working men became eligible to vote and as a result the labouring classes formed their own political party, called Labour, to challenge the old-established Conservatives and Liberals. By 1900 there were several Labour members of Parliament and these early socialists advocated a whole range of measures designed to assist the labouring classes who supported the new party. Workmen would, for the first time, be compensated by their employer if injured at work; miners would not be expected to work underground more than eight hours per day; Labour Exchanges were built to form a link between those seeking jobs and employers with vacancies to offer.

However, the most far-reaching measure was the Trade Disputes Act of 1906. This made it legal for individuals to act together as a Trade Union yet not be liable for damages arising from their actions; effectively giving unions immunity from the law and making the power to strike a very strong weapon. In many respects this was seen as a necessary counter-weight to factory-owners and large-scale farmers, many of whom had a monopoly of jobs and used this advantage to offer wages that were too low and conditions that were unfair.

Many of these Acts of Parliament, including the provision of a pension for those too old to work, were enacted by the Liberals who, aware of the growing electoral strength of the Labour Party, decided to carry forward the radicals flag themselves. Herbert Asquith had become Prime Minister in 1908 having succeeded Sir Henry Campbell-Bannerman, but the real Liberal driving force was a Welshman called David Lloyd-George.

Holding a number of influential government posts in rapid succession Lloyd-George waged financial war on the wealthy and privileged. He planned to increase their taxes to pay a higher rate of old-age pension, and to introduce a National Insurance Bill to provide state funds with which to pay workers who were sick or unemployed. For the first time women would receive a maternity grant when their children were born.

The House of Commons, with its majority of Liberal and Labour members, greeted this balancing act, of increased taxes and increased benefits, with enthusiasm. The House of Lords, with an in-built Conservative majority, were horrified and rejected Lloyd-George's proposals in 1909. The rejection was not welcomed by King Edward who thought the Upper House was being short-

sighted in precipitating a constitutional crisis: it had been accepted for generations that the House of Commons, as the *elected*
House, should not be denied its will on matters of real substance
and balancing the budget was certainly that. An election was
called and again the Liberals and Labour found themselves with a
House of Commons majority. Now the House of Lords felt a real
moral obligation to accept the re-submission of balancing a
budget favouring the working class at the expense of the wealthy.
Even so the constitutional damage had been done and Lloyd-
George—earning for himself the title of 'Welsh Wizard'—proposed that in future the (hereditary) House of Lords would no
longer have the power to veto over financial measures proposed
by the (elected) House of Commons and could only delay other
Acts for one year. In effect formalising a tacit understanding that
had existed for many many years but which the Lords had been
provoked into breaking. This reformation of the House of Lord's
duties was widely debated during 1910 (although the Parliament
Bill, as it was called, did not become law until the following year),
and in that same year King Edward the Seventh died; an
extrovert, even flamboyant king, who saw quite clearly the
dangers into which Europe was rushing headlong and who used
his position as 'Europe's uncle' in the service of his government
and his country. The Edwardian Era was short by Victorian
standards but it too was a watershed on the way to 1914.

King George the Fifth was thus immediately catapulted into a
major constitutional battle of Commons and People versus Lords
and their inherited privileges. Like William the Fourth, in similar
circumstances surrounding the 1832 Reform Bill, King George
threatened to swamp the House of Lords with radically-minded
peers if the Upper House refused to accept the clear intentions of
the people as expressed by their representatives in the House of
Commons. Not surprisingly the Lords capitulated as they had in
1832. The incident demonstrated yet again that the sovereign
would always act in support of the electorate's wishes, and it
made the cause of republicanism even less likely to succeed.

Several times in English history the eldest son had died before
his father and had escaped the responsibility of becoming king:
Henry the Second's eldest son (Henry) died before his father; so

did the Black Prince, eldest son of Edward the Third; so also did Prince Arthur, allowing his younger brother Henry to succeed as Henry the Eighth; Charles the First became king only because his older brother Henry died prior to their father James the First; and Prince Frederick died in 1751, nine years before his father, which allowed George the Third to reach the throne at a very early age. Likewise, Edward the Seventh's eldest son the Duke of Clarence died in 1892 so that the second son, George, had known for some time that he would eventually come to the throne as George the Fifth. An interesting parallel is that Prince Arthur married Katherine of Aragon who later married Henry the Eighth when Arthur died. Similarly, the Duke of Clarence was betrothed to Princess Mary (although death robbed them of a wedding) who then married George and so found herself in 1910 as Queen Mary, consort to King George the Fifth.

The new king was unlike his father in many respects; he was shy, disliked public engagements, and saw his role as similar to that of his grandmother, Queen Victoria, both in acting the part of a sober, correct and dutiful monarch, and as the head of an Empire that had been woefully neglected.

As a prince, King George had visited India, Canada and Australia and now he and Queen Mary visited India again. Having been crowned King of Great Britain in Westminster Abbey, it was thought diplomatically useful for the king to attend a ceremony in India—the Delhi Durbar—where King George would appear crowned as Emperor of India and a special crown was made (now part of the crown jewels) for this 1911 visit. King George and Queen Mary thus made a useful contribution to establishing Indian unity, binding that country closer to Great Britain, and reminding the wider British Empire that England's king was their king too.

At home in England the Liberals began to resurrect Gladstone's vision of Home Rule for Ireland, whilst at the same time many industrial workers were on strike, taking advantage of their immunity from the laws of contract and damages. Then, suddenly, the problems of Ireland and labour disputes were thrust aside as Europe plunged headlong into that four years of madness called The Great War, or The First World War.

The tragedy, the real tragedy, of 1914 is that none of the great powers had cause to quarrel with each other. Europe was enjoying its longest period of peace for centuries, there was no ideological rift between nations, no dispute concerning frontiers or possession of land. Every country except France, Switzerland and Portugal were monarchies with varying degrees of constitutional restraint; citizens of one country travelled freely across international borders and could exchange their currency or pay accounts in gold coins without difficulty. As the summer of 1914 approached, Great Britain was even beginning to accept the enlarged German navy as an irritant rather than a threat. It is true that Kaiser Wilhelm continued to be idiosyncratic and capable of diplomatic mismanagement but the rest of Europe was learning to live with that too.

Then, on 28th June 1914, Archduke Franz Ferdinand of Austria was assassinated by a slav revolutionary at Sarajevo in Bosnia (now Yugoslavia). The events that followed have been exhaustively analysed in countless history books but, to summarise briefly: Austria demanded that the neighbouring country of Serbia should now stop its agitation within Bosnia against Austria; Serbia refused to accept this ultimatum, even knowing that Germany was encouraging Austria to make unacceptable demands; on 28th July Austria declared war on Serbia and Russia began to mobilise her forces to assist Serbia; France voiced its intention of supporting Russia and on 3rd August Germany declared war on France and immediately violated Belgium's neutrality; Great Britain declared war on Germany the following day, 4th August, not to support either France or Russia but in an effort to protect Belgium. The Great War had begun.

What made such a terrible conflict possible was not alliances, binding countries together in common purpose should any of them be attacked, nor was it an arms race between nations that had got out of control. What made the war almost inevitable was the technique of military planners with their demonic timetables of mobilisation and their commitment to pursuing a programme they were unable to halt once certain decisions had been taken. Probably Kaiser Wilhelm did not want a war against France and Russia, and he most certainly did not intend to fight England.

Nevertheless, his casual and careless support for Austria had repercussions that someone more diplomatically-minded should have foreseen. Likewise, his approval for a strategy based on a pre-emptive strike across France's undefended border with neutral Belgium was shortsighted and full of risks. If Britain was not to lose all credibility and honour it had to act when German forces violated defenceless Belgium on 4th August 1914. To generations of Englishmen the Great War has always been sub-titled 'The Kaiser's War'.

Within days the small British army was rushed to France and Belgium; so insignificant was it that a rumour started that the Kaiser sneeringly called the army 'contemptible' and true to their nature of understatement, the soldiers cheerfully described themselves as 'the old contemptibles'. Nevertheless, the British army successfully stemmed the German military tide, fighting a rear-guard action which first slowed and then halted the German advance. Almost at once a stagnant line of trenches and fortifications stretched from the Belgium coast, part of which remained in German hands until the war ended, across France to the Swiss border. This became the rigid merciless killing-ground of French, British and German soldiers, soon to be joined by soldiers from almost every country in the British Empire.

In the east a vast Russian army had been mobilised but, badly equipped and trained, they endured defeat after defeat. Russia's traditional enemy, Turkey, entered the war in support of Germany and Italy also entered, but disregarding its treaty obligations Italy fought against Germany and her Austrian allies.

Thus the battle-lines of immobility were drawn early and, in 1915, an effort was made to break the deadlock. In a spectacular and imaginative enterprise the British, with considerable help from Australian and New Zealand forces, landed on Gallipolli: that part of Turkey which straddles the Dardanelle Channel connecting the Black Sea to the Mediterranean. The idea—brilliant in conception but disastrous in its management—was to make a surprise attack on Constantinople, knock Turkey out of the war and drive a wedge into central Europe. Due to ineptitude, muddle and poor leadership the venture failed. It had been the brainchild of a man who had served as Home Secretary in 1910 and who was now First Lord of the Admiralty, Winston Churchill; although blameless for what had happened, he was obliged to leave the government and await developments.

Another opportunity to gain a decisive victory away from the mud and water-filled shell-holes came the following year, in 1916. This time in a sphere where the British had traditionally gained her greatest victories: at sea.

Ever since 1914 the Royal Navy had waited for a chance to do battle with the German Imperial Navy and had successfully blockaded the German coast to deny Germany access to the open seas. Individual warships had slipped in and out but the blockade had kept Germany's main fleet inactive, until in May 1916, in the waters between Germany and Denmark—Jutland—the two navies met. Unfortunately the Battle of Jutland proved inconclusive, creating a controversy that has raged ever since. Could Britain's Royal Navy have used more initiative, taken greater risks, and pursued the Imperial Navy with more enthusiasm and to greater purpose? In spite of being relatively unscathed, the German fleet escaped back to their safe ports and remained there until the war ended, relying on submarines to attack allied shipping.

In 1915 all political parties had closed ranks to concentrate on winning the war. Now, in late 1916, a change of leadership and emphasis took place. Asquith was replaced as Prime Minister by Lloyd-George, a man recognised to have the determination and skill to unite Britain into a common purpose. After the failures of Gallipolli and Jutland to end the war by inflicting one heavy decisive defeat on Germany and her allies, a reassessment of British policy was called for.

There was, apparently, no alternative to confronting Germany across the trenches and barbed wire that disfigured so much of France and Belgium. The front-line generals demanded more men and resources for one assault after another, each one costing more British lives than the one before. Thousands upon thousands of soldiers found themselves mown down by accurate German machine gunners, and the appalling casualty lists made grim reading to those responsible for conducting the country's affairs. At the time it must have seemed as if England herself was bleeding to death. The men being slaughtered were not ignorant peasants, unskilled factory workers, nor were they malcontents poised to cause revolution. These brave young men were often the eldest sons of aristocratic families, cultured and enlightened; thousands were skilled and educated workers, steeped in a tradition of parliamentary democracy, cherishing their natural freedom as a birthright. This would be a generation hard to replace and many might claim this loss can be felt into the last quarter of the twentieth century.

The war had now become a total war as no other previous conflict in history had been.

Innocent civilians were killed in their beds as German airships—Zeppelins—began dropping bombs on London. Food shortages became acute as German U-boats sank not only British merchant ships but also unarmed steamers from neutral countries trading with Britain. It was this indiscriminate submarine warfare which finally provoked the United States into declaring war on Germany, although mobilising American strength and carrying it across the Atlantic would take time.

One result of Lloyd-George taking control of policy was his decision to appoint Winston Churchill as Minister for Munitions. Always eager to exploit new ideas with enthusiasm Churchill gave his full support to a development begun by an agricultural engineer in eastern England. This was an armoured vehicle capable of driving through mud and resisting machine-gun bullets by using caterpillar tracks instead of wheels. To disguise the machine's true purpose it was called a 'tank' and tank it has been called ever since. Although the tank was a great success when first used in strength at Cambrai in 1917 the opportunity to exploit its potential by using it *en masse* and punching a wide hole through the German lines was never taken. Like Gallipolli and Jutland Britain's misuse of the tank must be seen as another strategic error.

The Great War produced few national heroes in the mould of Marlborough, Nelson or Wellington. Perhaps the nearest approach to joining this elite circle was T.E. Lawrence; Lawrence of Arabia. This charismatic and controversial figure was not a military commander in the conventional sense, but using his personality and intimate knowledge of Arab aspirations he persuaded thousands of Arabs to attack the Turks occupying Palestine and Mesopitamia—roughly the region now known as Israel, Jordan, Syria and Iraq. In appearance he looked like an Arab and acted like one, exploiting to the full the hatred he knew the Arabs felt towards their traditional Turkish oppressors. By leading the Arabs in their successful guerrilla warfare, he enabled a small proportion of British soldiers to control virtually the whole Middle East, an area which had become very important due to the emerging oil industry and a need to protect the Suez Canal.

Although Field Marshall Douglas Haig was the British Army commander in France and Belgium during the critical years of 1916, 1917, 1918 and although he earned respect for his single-minded determination to attack the German line, rather than rely on a war of passive defence and attrition, he sustained too many casualties to be widely admired. Even Lloyd-George, an inspirational war-time leader frequently dubbed 'the man who won the war' was too often seen to be a political opportunist, with motives that merely fed his personal ambition.

Thus, at the end of 1917, Britain found herself doing the very thing it enjoyed the least: fighting an all-out war, on land, against strong opponents, without the freedom to withdraw, make peace, or act independently—not that such courses of action were ever contemplated. The unpalatable fact was that England was in danger of destroying the very social and economic fabric it had created during many many centuries.

14

DEPRESSION AND DEFIANCE (1918 to 1951)

In 1918 the Great War ended; at the eleventh hour of the eleventh day of the eleventh month. The date and time have become an easily-remembered litany to perhaps the most futile and unnecessary war in modern history, a war that invites feelings of revulsion, horror and anger even now. It ended when Germany, crippled by food shortages and a morale near to collapse, decided on one last desperate attack which if successful would snatch a victory and gain at least an honourable peace. The gamble failed and in November Germany requested an armistice.

For the victors there were no spoils to be divided, only the dead to be buried and the economic cost evaluated. At the peace conference in Versailles some effort was made to make Germany pay for its misdeeds in the form of reparations, to be enforced by a physical occupation of its heavy industrial factories. This idea was quickly abandoned when it became clear that Germany was bankrupt, torn by internal revolt and incapable of repaying anyone anything. It was decided to create a demilitarised zone within the borders of Germany, the Rhineland between the River Rhine and the French border. For a time British and French soldiers occupied the area and they became known as The Watch on the Rhine. The Kaiser had already been despatched to a life of sweet retirement in Holland, leaving behind a republican vacuum of power that Adolf Hitler would eventually fill.

A similar fate was in store for the Austro-Hungarian Empire which disintegrated into a number of small republics. Serbia and Bosnia lost their identities when the Balkan map was redrawn and a whole host of newly-created countries claimed a spurious nationhood for themselves. Russia had shaken itself to its foundations by a revolution, and Turkey was stripped of the Ottoman Empire it had so cruelly and inefficiently administered for many centuries. Italy, although on the winning side, had suffered loss of pride by deploying an army unfit for battle and soon fell prey to Mussolini and his fascist blackshirts. Belgian neutrality was again restored behind borders still too weakly defended to resist a determined aggressor. France had every reason to be proud of enduring the war with courage, but she quickly lapsed into a weary apathy, losing all appetite for continuing as a world-power. America returned to her isolationism across the Atlantic, content to allow an ineffective League of Nations to maintain peace, even when a revitalised Germany was later seen to be embracing a vile form of National Socialism and threatening the free democracies again.

But, what of England?

Morale had remained high in spite of deprivations at home and mounting casualties at the battle grounds. All the institutions of monarchy and parliamentary democracy had survived stronger than ever. An immediate general election had confirmed Lloyd-George as Prime Minister, even though he would need the support of some Conservatives to maintain his government.

Soldiers from the trenches came home feeling that they had earned something from society; a popular expression at the time was that 'England must become a country fit for heroes'. Farm workers who had tolerated unfavourable working conditions for low pay in 1914 now expected improvements; factory hands took it for granted that full-employment was here to stay, and the army of servants and maids who had worked long hours serving the aristocratic families in their grand houses preferred to swell the ranks of those enjoying a more rewarding life in factories, shops and the transport industries that had expanded during the war. The England of 1918 was no longer the England of 1914 if only because the general population now had greater aspirations for themselves and their children. Every adult male—except those in prison, certified as insane, or who were peers of the realm—now had a vote in both local and national elections, and women aged thirty were also eligible to vote. For several years more the suffragettes continued to agitate, and break the law when necessary, to ensure that all adult women shared in the same universal suffrage as men. That eventually the government gave way and granted all women the vote in 1928 was due entirely to the determination of Emmeline Pankhurst, a veritable firebrand in the cause of women's emancipation.

For a time full-employment created an air of peaceful prosperity, and this gave the government a respite to deal with two major problems overseas.

The first concerned India. Vague demands for self-determination had been surfacing for a number of years but now a brilliant lawyer-turned-politician articulated these demands more cogently than before. Mahatma Gandhi was a pacifist who almost invented 'civil disobedience'. His cause seemed to be justified in 1919 when British soldiers used their guns against unarmed protesters in the city of Amritsar, and although a semblence of stability returned to India when Gandhi was imprisoned, a tidal wave of nationalism leading to eventual British withdrawal had started and could be slowed-down but not halted.

The second problem was the everlasting question of Ireland. Gladstone, and his Liberal successors prior to the Great War, had aroused hopes and expectations among Irish republicans which gained momentum with every year that passed. Even in Queen Victoria's reign the Irish patriots—Fenians—exploded bombs in London to underline their demands for Home Rule. In 1916 an armed uprising in Dublin was suppressed only when the British army used military force. The problem was exacerbated by the Protestant minority in Northern Ireland who threatened a counter-revolution if they were to be subjected to government from Dublin by the Catholic majority.

In 1920 the violence within Ireland assumed the proportion of war and it was evident that a solution to satisfy the South Irish majority must be found. This proved to be partitioning Ireland into two separate countries; the larger (southern) part, almost entirely republican-catholics, would be constituted as a self-governing state owing allegiance neither to Great Britain nor King George, to be called Eire. The small area of six counties—Northern Ireland, or Ulster—inhabited by Protestants loyal to King George but with a sizeable Catholic majority, would remain within the United Kingdom. This solution, although far from ideal, was acceptable to almost all Irishmen, except for a section of hard-core Irish republicans who wanted the whole of Ireland ruled from Dublin. The problem of unification has defied all attempts by men of goodwill to 'square the circle', and outbreaks of violence by the self-styled Irish Republican Army has continued ever since, echoed by their violent counterparts from within the Protestant north who attack Catholics with equal ferocity.

If India and Ireland were anxious to gain some form of 'freedom' the same could not be said of the British Empire as a whole. Canada, Australia, New Zealand and a score of other territories had become more and more loyal to King George the Fifth and the 'Mother Country'; finding that radio, combined with the first faltering steps of long-distance air travel, seemed to bind Great Britain and her Empire even closer together. South Africa was just as loyal; indeed one of her statesmen, General Smuts, an Afrikaaner who had fought against Britain during the Boer War, had given England much useful service throughout the Great War.

Great Britain was now to find herself in need of friends as an economic crisis engulfed the world.

For a short time, during the transition from war to peace, England enjoyed a brief period of full employment. The upper classes seemed as privileged as before, in spite of Lloyd-George's attempts to tax their accumulated wealth. The middle classes acquired motor cars, telephones and began to venture into France, Germany and Italy for their holidays. As for the working classes, they too began to benefit from improved social conditions and opportunities for better education. Only the very poor seemed unable to break their bonds of environmental poverty. At this moment a world-wide recession plunged all modern industrial countries into a depressing circle of unemployment leading to reduced demand for manufacturing goods, leading to more unemployment.

By 1924 Great Britain had 20% of its workforce unemployed, and this gradually worsened year by year. A move to stimulate demand by cutting the pay of coal miners led to a General Strike in 1926 but this proved short-lived when the middle and upper classes maintained essential services, forcing the trade unions to accept defeat. The economic depression—in Britain it was known as 'the slump'—brought mass-unemployment and great hardship to the north of England especially, where the heavy industries almost came to a standstill. Many of the unemployed marched 300 miles to London in an effort to persuade Parliament into adopting policies that would provide work and stimulate trade.

Nevertheless, there was no violent reaction to what was seen as governmental complacency. Communism found little support anywhere in Europe, even though Russia had begun exporting its own political creed with missionary zeal. Capitalism was under strain but to many it was preferable to any alternative, and in due course Franklin Delano Roosevelt became President of the United States, slowly reversing the trend of depression there. This had an effect in most other countries and gradually confidence was restored as factories started employing more workers.

In Britain during the Twenties and Thirties politics changed to reflect first the mood of economic crisis and then the feeling that events were becoming more favourable. Lloyd-George and his Liberals were obliged to give way to Ramsey Macdonald, the Labour party's first Prime Minister. He led a government comprising elements from all political groupings, although some members of the Labour party saw this as a betrayal of his socialist principles and a split developed and widened within the movement. Stanley Baldwin, leader of the Conservative party, was the next Prime Minister but, because neither Labour nor Conservatives could command a parliamentary majority, Ramsey Macdonald and Stanley Baldwin alternated as Prime Minister over a 'government of national unity' until 1935, when the Conservatives under first Stanley Baldwin and then Neville Chamberlain formed a government from within their own political party.

Baldwin was a placid pipe-smoking man who exuded confidence and complacency, presiding like a benign uncle over a country where the middle and working classes could again begin to think of raising their standard of living. New housing programmes and an improved welfare system offered most people a safety net preventing wholesale poverty on the Victorian scale.

Only Winston Churchill—out of political office since expressing his disagreement with government policy on disarmament and what he regarded as undue haste in moving towards self-rule for India—struck a discordant note. Again and again he voiced warnings about what he saw happening in Germany, Spain and Italy. In all these countries fascist dictatorships were threatening Europe's fragile peace. Germany in particular began to take advantage of French and British weakness as Hitler marched his soldiers into the demilitarised Rhineland and ignored the Treaty of Versailles limiting the size of Germany's armed forces.

In any case England was now diverted by its own constitutional crisis, one that threatened to divide the country.

On 20th January, 1936, King George the Fifth died, to be succeeded by his eldest son who took the title of Edward the Eighth. The new king had previously managed to undertake his princely duties diligently whilst revealing his addiction for a life of frivolous entertainment, and he began his reign on a tidal wave of immense popularity. King Edward was charming, handsome, and unmarried. It soon became clear that he particularly enjoyed the company of an American, Mrs Wallace Simpson, who was about to be divorced from her American husband. When the king announced his intention of marrying Mrs Simpson a constitutional crisis became inevitable; as Head of the Church of England the king had standards to meet and conventions to be observed. Neither the cabinet, government, nor Parliament could accept the King of England marrying a divorcee and in December 1936, amidst debate and differences of opinion throughout Great Britain and the Empire, the king abdicated rather than given way.

Thus Edward's younger brother came to the throne as King George the Sixth, and his wife Queen Elizabeth, together with their two daughters, Elizabeth and Margaret, restored stability and a home-spun popularity to the throne of England.

Not even King George's coronation in the summer of 1937, with all its pageantry and release of loyal sentiments from the British Empire, could hide the unpalatable truth that Adolf Hitler was beginning to constitute a real threat within Europe.

In 1938 Neville Chamberlain made a number of journies to Germany, hoping that he could dissuade Hitler from action which would lead to war. Chamberlain has since been accused of appeasement by allowing Hitler to seize control of Austria and Czechoslovakia. Others claim he bought valuable time during which Great Britain started to build its defences. Certainly, after the Prime Minister's final meeting with Hitler in Munich, during October 1938, rearmament was seen to be both necessary and urgent. Civil Defence, including the building of air raid shelters, was given high priority; so too was the new generation of fighter aircraft to intercept enemy bombers; both Spitfires and Hurricanes were produced in fair numbers as young men volunteered to fly them. Ship builders who had built the two great transatlantic liners, Queen Mary and Queen Elizabeth, found themselves with orders to modernise the Royal Navy. At the same time motor car manufacturers began to satisfy government demands for tanks and other armoured vehicles.

On 1st September 1939 Germany invaded Poland, refusing to withdraw when Britain demanded they should. Two days later Great Britain declared war on Germany; not because of any attack on its own territory but, as in 1914, because Germany was seen to be bullying a weaker neighbour and Britain felt obliged to intervene.

In 1914 there had been enthusiasm, even jubilation at the prospect of going to war and teaching the Kaiser a lesson. In 1939 the mood was rather more sober. Public buildings had already been protected by sand-bags. Now air-raid shelters stood on many street corners, and trenches dug across the royal parks of London. This would be a war involving civilians as much as soldiers, sailors and airmen. Schoolchildren were evacuated to the safety of England's countryside and gas masks issued to everyone. Great Britain prepared herself for attack, aware that Germany was militarily stronger and capable of using its strength more ruthlessly.

For six months very little happened. Poland was quickly defeated and occupied; a peace treaty between Germany and Russia enabled Hitler to concentrate his efforts in the west, which, in the spring of 1940, he attacked with an efficiency reflecting campaign successes in Poland. Tanks and infantry, supported by airplanes used as an additional tactical weapon, poured over the French border and swept across Belgian neutrality like a re-run of

1914.

This time the French offered less resistance and German tanks ensured a war of rapid movement and not stagnation. British soldiers, again in Belgium as they had been in 1914, struggled to hold back an invincible tide without success. In May 1940 the British army withdrew from continental Europe, rescued from the beaches of Dunkirk by a flotilla of small boats that continually risked death and destruction to bring Britain's army back to England's south coast. If any retreat can be called a victory, then Dunkirk most certainly was.

Germany devoured not only Belgium, Holland, Denmark and Norway but also France; part to be occupied by German forces and part to be administered by the French, but in accordance with German policy and demands. An unhappy situation for a country with France's greatness and past history. Britain did try to assist Norway by sending elements from all three branches of the armed forces; it proved to be a hopeless task and critics at the time said it was a classic case of 'too little and too late'.

Neville Chamberlain, a decent patriotic Englishman, was clearly not the man to lead Britain at a time when the country was beginning to stare at the possibility of defeat. Onto this stage walked Winston Churchill, as if he had been waiting all his life for this one great challenge. Facing a determined and powerful enemy, only twenty miles distant across the English Channel, Churchill offered no easy solutions, only the 'blood, sweat and tears' of people he knew would not be easily beaten. Germany, and German sympathisers, held very nearly the whole of continental Europe, a feat without parallel in recent military history. Its submarines prowled beneath the sea around England; its airplanes poised to launch a bombing attack on every city and town within range. Only at sea did Britain hold any advantage, and this a slender one. Again and again the Royal Navy actively sought its German counterpart, cornering and sinking individual battleships like the *Graf Spee*, but unable to bring its experience and tradition to a sea-battle with Germany's main surface fleet, the result of which might possibly have had strategic repercussions. Instead a new tradition was created by men wearing a uniform of a lighter shade of blue, this time in the skies of

England itself.

During the summer of 1940 Germany launched its bombers with fighter escort onto targets in Southern England. Spitfires and Hurricanes, flown by pilots little older than overgrown school-boys, held the defensive line protecting London from total destruction. The line became thread-bare at times as British losses mounted and reserves of men and machines sank dangerously low. August gave way to September and the Germans renewed their daytime attacks with increasing numbers, until their losses were judged by Hitler to be unacceptable and to England's audible sigh of relief the battle was abandoned. Churchill had anticipated the struggle for air supremacy and had called it The Battle of Britain. Paying fulsome tribute to the young airmen he declared: 'Never in the field of human conflict was so much owed by so many to so few'. Those Royal Air Force pilots always remained proud of being 'The Few'.

As one battle ended another began. Germany transferred its bomber offensive from daylight to night attacks. For the next three years every major city was in the frontline of what became known as 'the blitz'. London, Coventry, Plymouth, Hull, Birming-ham, Bristol and Glasgow all endured a nightly reign of terror. So too did Sheffield, Manchester and Liverpool. Shortages of food, fuel, indeed of everything, made life difficult but not intolerable. Rationing was fair and seen to be fair. People living through this period, sharing danger and disaster together, claimed it was the most rewarding episode of their lives. Surveying the whole of English History, Churchill could safely declare this period as Britain's 'Finest Hour'.

Fearing invasion each and every day the coastline was given extra defences, and all able bodied men too old to serve in the regular armed forces volunteered for part-time army duties, ready to fight when necessary. Called the Home Guard but earning the nickname 'Dad's Army' they may appear comical now, but in 1940 and 1941 they were a reminder of Churchill's pledge: 'We shall fight on the beaches, we shall fight in the fields and in the streets, we shall fight in the hills; we shall never surrender'.

In the summer of 1941 Germany invaded Russia and a few months later Japan made a surprise attack on the American base

of Pearl Harbour. America promptly declared war on both Japan
and Germany, whilst Britain added Japan to her list of enemies.
This was becoming a global war in which the democracies found
themselves ranged against forces that were judged to be evil and
which must be defeated if civilisation were to survive.

As during the 1914-18 war it took time for America to mobilise
itself fully, suffering many defeats in the Pacific theatre. Britain
itself endured the loss of Singapore, with Japanese soldiers cutting
through Burma towards the rich prize of India. However every
country in the British Empire had been supporting Great Britain
from the beginning and slowly the tide of enemy advances began
to ebb.

Without doubt the turning point of the war for England
occurred in October 1942 at El Alamein, not so very far from
Alexandria and the Suez canal. German troops—the famous
Afrika Korp—under Rommel had driven the British army back
until there was little room for further retreat. The Desert
Army—they called themselves 'the desert rats'—now acquired a
new leader in General Bernard Montgomery, and he led his army
to a victory the English had been yearning for. Montgomery—
Monty—was outwardly flamboyant and charismatic in the manner of Nelson and Wellington. He quickly became popular with
the general public and was unashamedly hero-worshipped by his
own soldiers. He was also cautious by nature and reluctant to risk
men's lives unnecessarily. When Montgomery launched the Battle
of El Alamein he revealed his generalship in triumphant fashion,
driving Rommel and his Afrika Korp out of North Africa in one
long continuous battle. It is said that 'before El Alamein we never
had a victory, after it we never had a defeat'. In November of that
year, 1942, Churchill put it this way: 'This is not the end. It is not
even the beginning of the end. But it is, perhaps, the end of the
beginning'.

With a unified command structure of Americans and British
together, first Sicily, then Italy, was invaded and in June 1944 the
long awaited invasion of Western Europe took place under the
overall command of General Eisenhower. Russia had withstood
the seige of Stalingrad and was pushing the Germans back with
increasing speed, thus the two mighty armies of Russia in the east,

and combined Americans, British and their allies in the west, crushed Germany to defeat. Only when the Nazi concentration camps were liberated was the full horror of that regime appreciated, and if ever justification was needed for Britain's sacrifice and decision to wage war on Hitler's Germany, the roll call of Dachau, Belsen and Auschwitz provided it.

Germany was forced into unconditional surrender on 7th May 1945, a day to be remembered as VE Day (Victory in Europe Day) and celebrated with much rejoicing on the streets of London as elsewhere. King George, Queen Elizabeth, Princess Elizabeth in her army uniform, and Princess Margaret were joined on the balcony of Buckingham Palace by Britain's architect of victory, Winston Churchill. By his inspired leadership, at a time when Britain seemed to be on the brink of defeat, Churchill at the age of 70 could fairly be described as England's 'Man of the Century'. It was doubly fortunate that he had developed a personal friendship with President Roosevelt long before becoming Prime Minister. This enabled the two men to correspond together in intimate terms, sharing confidences in a manner seldom achieved by international leaders and England benefited by receiving from America much military and economic assistance in 1940 and 1941, a time when practical help proved most useful.

President Roosevelt died in April 1945 before he could appreciate the fruits of victory. He was succeeded as President by Harry Truman, a true friend of Britain yet lacking that personal involvement which had made the Roosevelt-Churchill relationship so special. All the campaigns in Europe had been fought with Britain almost an equal partner with her more powerful cousin, America. In the Pacific, America was undoubtedly the senior partner and it was America's decision to bring an immediate end to the war by dropping an atomic bomb first on Hiroshima and then Nagasaki. So, on 12th September 1945, VJ Day (Victory against Japan) was celebrated as the Second World War came to an end.

Between VE and VJ Days Britain held a general election to decide which political party and leader would dismantle the guns and beat them into ploughshares. In spite of his massive achievements, and very real popularity, Churchill's party—the Conservatives—was heavily defeated and Labour, under Clement Attlee as Prime Minister, had a clear majority in Parliament.

It seems now like a stroke of unimaginable confidence that in 1944 the British government planned a major overhaul of its entire educational system, to raise the school-leaving age to 15 and to encourage a voluntary higher level beyond that. The credit for such planning went to a rising young Conservative R.A. Butler, a man destined to hold every political appointment except that of Prime Minister. At the same time, indeed slightly earlier, the keen brain of William Beveridge produced a comprehensive welfare system that went far beyond the elementary steps taken by Lloyd-George thirty years before, a scheme in advance of any country except the outright communism of Soviet Russia.

Labour, under Prime Minister Attlee, set their first sights on implementing both Butler's Education Act of 1944 and the many facets of what was known as the Beveridge Plan: Even more comprehensive systems of national insurance and welfare benefits were introduced but the main element was a Health Service giving everyone in the country free hospital and dental treatment, free medicine, and free consultation with doctors whose fees would be paid directly by the state. Coal mines and the railway system were taken into public ownership, so were many other industries and public utilities; all of this taking place during the first five years of peace, so quickly that the country found itself knee-deep in socialism almost before the armed forces began to be disbanded.

Such disbandment, when it came, was exceedingly brief.

During the closing years of the war a series of conferences by the leaders of America, Britain and Russia had decided on the world's future direction. Winston Churchill expressed unease at the way in which Stalin was being granted a blank cheque allowing Russia's Red Army to influence the politics of Eastern Europe: Poland, Hungary, Rumania etc. Nevertheless, either Churchill did not voice his fears strongly enough or he judged that 1943 and 1944 were not the years to protest at what might or might not happen several years into the future. Russia was a vital ally in the fight against a common enemy, and Roosevelt was idealist enough not to share Churchill's doubts and uncertainties.

The post-war period of harmony between Russia and the west was short and in 1948 America and Britain took a determined stand when Russia closed the land border with Berlin, forcing that city to be fed and fuelled by a massive airlift. Even earlier, on 5th March 1946, in the American city of Fulton, Winston Churchill described the shutter coming down between Russia and her wartime allies as an 'iron curtain'; it proved to be a memorably accurate description.

With great reluctance Britain re-introduced conscription, making it compulsory for young men to join the armed forces for a period that was sometimes eighteen months, sometimes two years.

During this post-war period the British Empire began to fall neatly into two camps. Those dominions with traditionally white Anglo-Saxon settlers who wanted to continue governing themselves and yet remain culturally close to 'the Mother country', putting themselves in the same relationship to the king as England; countries such as Canada, Australia and New Zealand. Others wanted to remain within the loose Commonwealth structure and yet break free from Britain and become totally independent at the very first opportunity; India and several African countries were in this group.

India was granted full independence during 1947, although the actual event was messy, bloody, and indicated that impatience in seizing their freedom was not always beneficial. The subcontinent immediately split into two separate countries; India (largely populated by those sharing the Hindu faith) and Pakistan (almost entirely Muslim). A third fragment (Bangladesh) broke away later, demonstrating perhaps that British rule had been almost miraculous in retaining such a high degree of unification for so long.

It became British policy that no country would be forced to remain part of the Commonwealth if it demonstrated that self-government was desired by a majority of the population, and that such government was capable of adminstering itself. Many black-African countries expressed a wish to be independent and the hauling down of the British flag and its replacement by one of unfamiliar design became a frequent occurrence, and in most cases strong economic and cultural ties have remained. The Union of South Africa did not achieve full independence until 1961, declaring itself a republic and severing all formal links with Great Britain whilst keeping many traditions to remind them of their Anglo-Saxon origins.

The dismantlement of what was once the British Empire, and its replacement by a Commonwealth of forty countries, each recognising the British sovereign as its head, closed another chapter in England's long history, and in 1951 the future looked as uncertain as all futures inevitably look.

15

By 1951 the British electorate had tasted six years of socialism and wanted a change. So, at the age of 77, Winston Churchill became Prime Minister again when he led the Conservatives to victory.

Nevertheless, Labour's six years had transformed the social and economic life of Britain, setting a pattern that would remain intact for another thirty years. Clement Attlee, a quiet, thoughtful, and exceedingly modest Prime Minister does not fit the popular image of a stereotype radical, yet he presided over a Labour government determined to change the system of managing the country's affairs. Railways, coal mines, steel production, important sections of heavy industry together with the provision of gas and electricity were now in public ownership, an integral part of the state's management of its economy. So too were hospitals, doctors and dentists, offering to the entire population a free service ranging from major surgical operations to cough drops. The National Health Service was so comprehensive and all-embracing it became, almost overnight, the envy of many countries who began to emulate the Labour government's greatest achievement.

The Health Service was supported by such an array of pensions, allowances and other benefits, that it was no exaggeration to claim every man, woman and child enjoyed a large measure of social security 'from the cradle to the grave'.

A few months before the smooth transfer of power from Labour to Conservative came the 1951 Festival of Britain. This was an anniversary celebration of Prince Albert's 1851 Great Exhibition and was intended as a national showcase to demonstrate that, as in 1851, Britain could lead the world in technology and inventiveness. The Festival was also a feast of pleasure and entertainment, a reminder that the country had emerged victorious from war and should, optimistically, be looking forward to an era of peace and prosperity.

On the surface Great Britain's mood was buoyant and relaxed. Motor cars were in mass-production again and within the financial reach of many families, for the more adventurous a wide choice of British-made motor cycles filled many showrooms; volume sales of cars and motor cycles at home being shared with a flourishing export trade to the Commonwealth and United States especially. Much the same story was true of furniture, china and labour-saving household appliances. The television service, pioneered for a brief period before the war, had fully resumed and Frank Whittle's invention of the jet engine was paving the way for Britain to build the world's first civil jet airliner; the Comet. Britain seemed poised to recapture a lion's share of the world's trade, both in the new technology of air and television equipment, and also in the mass-production of almost everything else. Past experience and new inventiveness gave the nation an advantage only America could equal.

Unfortunately, Britain's heavy industry and manufacturing plants had become hopelessly inefficient and out-of-date. A lack of capital investment and the continuation of old-fashioned working practices by an over-unionised labour force would, in time, lead to the decline of Britain's economy. However, during the 1950's and early 1960's, the country basked in the glow of full-employment, rising living standards and the comforting safety-net of a state-funded welfare system. These attractive conditions encouraged an influx of migrant workers from India, Pakistan and the Caribbean, all of them taking advantage of their Commonwealth status to settle in Britain with their children and parental dependents. The social consequences of large ethnic groups forming enclaves within English cities were slow to be appreciated.

Almost as slow to be appreciated as the distasteful fact that Britain was losing its competitive advantage in the world's market place. Germany and Japan had both made spectacular recoveries from the ravages of war and neither had burdened themselves with expensive welfare systems. Their labour force worked long hours in new modern factories to produce well-designed goods that were soon out-selling their British equivalents. Adding to Britain's competitive problems were the cheap labour-markets of many far-east countries, workers performing repetitive, unskilled tasks in return for exceedingly low wages.

By tradition the English have prospered as craftsmen, inventors, specialists in any activity that requires flair and imagination; from colonising virgin territory to creating a banking and insurance empire centred on the one square mile of the City of London. What the English dislike is the very idea of being slaves, subservient either to a despotic king, fascist dictator, or a factory assembly line with its soul-destroying repetition. British workmanship and inventive genius were seen to advantage when the great liner Queen Elizabeth 2 (Q.E.2) was launched, and later when the Hovercraft and Harrier jumpjet were developed. Rolls Royce had few rivals in the field of hand-built cars or sophisticated aero-engines, but in the vital market for mass-produced cars, motor cycles and other machine-made goods Britain began to lose ground to her more efficient competitors. This loss of business did not happen with dramatic suddenness but over a period of years. Nevertheless it was a loss that pointed to an irreversible trend.

Thus Winston Churchill became Prime Minister at a time when economic problems lay slightly into the future, yet the early portents of decline were, with hindsight, all too evident. His Conservative Party colleagues had opposed Labour's creation of a welfare state and the public ownership of hitherto private companies, yet Churchill was shrewd enough to judge that his Conservatives had been returned to power to manage the existing system more efficiently rather than dismantle what Attlee and his socialists had achieved. This principle would remain Conservative philosophy until the advent of Margaret Thatcher in 1979.

Meanwhile the 1951 Festival of Britain gave everyone a comfortable feeling and an excuse to celebrate an end to wartime austerity and the arrival of peace and plenty.

It came as a shock on 6th February 1952 when the nation learned that King George the Sixth had died peacefully in his sleep, even though his ill-health had been apparent during his most recent public engagements. His eldest daughter, Princess Elizabeth, hurriedly returned home from Kenya accompanied by her Greek-born husband, Prince Philip. The new queen became the very first English sovereign not to know the exact time when she assumed her royal title and duties, because the precise time of King George's death was not known.

Queen Elizabeth the Second was crowned in Westminster Abbey on 2nd June 1953 in a ceremony of much traditional splendour and pageantry. She was exceptionally popular, already with a young son as heir to the throne, Charles, and her husband had shown himself to be intelligent and outspoken in a manner denied to reigning kings and queens. The advent of Queen Elizabeth the Second gave rise to much misplaced popular sentiment concerning the 'New Elizabethans' and invoking the ghosts of Drake, Raleigh and England's first Queen Elizabeth, to inspire a revival of the country's enterprising spirit.

Two years later, in 1955, Churchill decided to retire as Prime Minister; he was a gifted writer, historian, painter with above-average talent, a politician who although first elected to Parliament in 1900 as a Conservative, switched to Liberalism almost immediately afterwards, and held his first government appointment in 1906 before political fortunes swept him back into the Conservative ranks and to his eventual walk with destiny.

The new Prime Minister, Sir Anthony Eden, was both distinguished and debonair, very experienced in foreign affairs and sharing Churchill's pre-war condemnation of all European dictatorships. In little more than a year Eden made a tragic miscalculation and found himself in a crisis and controversy that continues to raise arguments even now.

In November 1956 Colonel Nasser, Egypt's new ruler, seized control of the Suez Canal and placed limitations on who could or could not use it. This was contrary to international agreement and as both France and Great Britain were the joint administrators of the canal they could not ignore Nasser's challenge. Accordingly they despatched a combined force of paratroopers and a seaborne invading army to occupy the Canal Zone and protect it from a threatened attack by Israel. Critics claimed the Israeli threat was merely a pretext and that Britain, France and Israel were in collusion to deny Egypt control of an important waterway wholly within Egyptian territory.

The military operation was efficient and successful but it brought condemnation from America, Russia and almost every other country. In Parliament the Labour opposition voiced their denunciation and in response to all the pressure Sir Anthony Eden withdrew the British army with as much dignity as he could muster. This incident drove Sir Anthony Eden to an early retirement but the Conservative majority in Parliament remained secure, and their new party leader, Harold Macmillan, assumed the mantle of Prime Minister as a matter of course.

Harold Macmillan proved himself to be one of the most skilfull and articulate of all Prime Ministers; the newspaper cartoonists soon depicted him as 'Supermac', flying over his problems with outstretched arms. Britain's economic situation continued to decline as a succession of high wage claims, unrelated to productivity, superficially raised living standards at the expense of money borrowed to bridge the deficit. Nevertheless, Harold Macmillan declared to Britain's labour force the memorable phrase 'You have never had it so good!' His comment was apt and all too true; the tragedy is that the consequences of high wages and low productivity were foreseen by economists and politicians alike and yet little was done to check the rate of inflation that would shortly become one of the highest in Europe. Not for another twenty years would the problem be met head-on, and only then at a cost of massive unemployment.

It is both unfair and incorrect to suggest that all the economic ills of Britain in the period 1956-1980 were due to a work-force using the strike weapon to extort high wages from an economy unable to pay without borrowing. Britain was deploying an army, navy and air force in defence of western Europe far beyond her economic means, its expensive welfare schemes were frequently abused and bureaucratically mismanaged, but also its cost of imported middle-east oil began rising faster than Great Britain could produce goods to pay for it. As a trading nation, with the pound sterling an internationally-quoted currency, the reality of borrowing to balance the books was a serious matter that directly affected the world's confidence in Britain.

In 1963 Harold Macmillan became seriously ill and his successor as leader of the Conservative Party (and therefore as Prime Minister) was not obvious. In a move that some regarded as constitutionally controversial Queen Elizabeth appointed Lord Home as Prime Minister, having first consulted senior members of the Conservative Party. It was a decision that prompted the party in future to adopt Labour's policy of electing their own leader and thus make the sovereign's duty of appointing the Prime Minister more straightforward.

The following year, 1964, Harold Wilson led Labour to an electoral victory ending, in his own words 'thirteen years of Tory misrule'. As Prime Minister he wrestled with the twin problems of curbing trade union power and of reducing wage demands that were getting higher and higher; always remembering that the Labour Party drew its strength and inspiration from the working-class element of society. He also looked across the English Channel and observed what was happening there.

France, Belgium, Germany, Holland and Italy formed themselves into a loosely-knit union which was designed to assist trade between themselves whilst, at the same time, making it difficult for other countries to sell goods to them. This grouping fell short of political unity or any degree of federalism; the object was to reduce restrictions to trade between themselves and to make border crossings by goods and travelling individuals easier. Britain had been invited to join many years earlier, sharing her experience and technology with her continental neighbours, but the offer was declined, partly because of trade links with the old empire and also to preserve the country's traditional independence in matters of trade and economics.

The European Common Market (E.E.C.) grew in strength and prosperity whilst Britain declined, and Harold Wilson made the first tentative steps to secure entry to the Common Market. France, in the person of her President, General de Gaulle, was less than enthusiastic and effectively vetoed Britain's entry; principally because Britain had not entered from the very beginning and had thus shown an unwelcome reluctance to be regarded as 'good Europeans'.

Meanwhile Harold Wilson and Labour were no more successful than earlier governments in halting the country's economic downhill slide. In 1970 Edward Heath became Prime Minister when the Conservatives regained office. The change from Labour to Conservative government failed to produce any sort of economic miracle, but Edward Heath did succeed in persuading the E.E.C. to allow Great Britain to join them as full members. By now the European Community had become more sophisticated and more ambitious, and the degree of consensus between participating states had become stronger, even to the extent of making 'European Laws' in the form of regulations that individual countries were expected to implement through their own parliaments. As a dedicated 'European', Edward Heath used all his diplomatic skill to end Great Britain's isolation and in 1973 he was rewarded when his signature was added to The Treaty of Rome; this was the document embracing all terms and conditions of E.E.C membership.

Whether Edward Heath's diplomacy was appreciated by all Englishmen quickly became a subject for debate. The overwhelming majority recognised the Common Market as being vital to Britain's economic survival, although there was little enthusiasm nor very much rejoicing. A few nurtured idealist visions of a United States of Europe, with a common currency, common laws enacted by one European Parliament, and no internal frontiers between Common Market members. These visionaries however, were a distinct minority.

Membership of the E.E.C. did not prove to be an instant cure-all for Britain's problems and in 1974 Edward Heath's decision to deny the coal miners a wage increase the industry claimed it could not afford, led to a strike in every coal-field. This reduced output from the power stations, and factories throughout the country could operate on only three days each week. The crisis obliged Edward Heath to ask Queen Elizabeth for a dissolution of Parliament and new elections returned Harold Wilson and Labour to office.

Neither Harold Wilson, nor his successor James Callaghan, could resolve the equation of high wage claims leading to rising inflation, leading in turn to higher wage claims. Even the discovery of massive oil and gas deposits in the seas around Britain could not, by themselves, rectify the economic imbalance. Nor would it be resolved by new technology which provided a whole catalogue of useful scientific achievements; of which the world's first supersonic airliner Concorde, (developed jointly with France), and a range of advanced nuclear power stations, are the best known examples. These achievements, and many more besides, had to be discounted by broadly overpriced labour costs which discouraged investment in new industry.

By 1979 many people came to recognise that Great Britain was approaching a crossroads in her destiny, an instinctive feeling that only a radical change in policy and philosophy could reverse the depressing trend. Margaret Thatcher, who had displaced Edward Heath as leader of the Conservatives, personified this desire for change and when Labour were defeated in a parliamentary vote of no-confidence she won the subsequent general election to become Britain's first woman Prime Minister. The scene was now set for some profound rethinking and a reappraisal of the direction Great Britain had been taking since 1945.

Whether or not this change of direction will prove successful is too early to say, but it can be said with some certainty that two factors will remain constant. The first is the geographical location of Britain as an island, and secondly the character of its people.

By nature and force of circumstance island-people are conditioned to be insular, and to survive they must be prepared to defend themselves against all invaders. England has done this, but has also been adventurous enough to explore, colonise, and exert a cultural influence on countries far larger than herself. Because the English cherish their own freedom they have been quick to defend the freedom of others, sometimes at great personal cost to themselves, and this desire to be born free and remain free has run like a thread through the tapestry of English History. English law and English parliamentary democracy have been models for the world to copy; neither institution is perfect but both are infinitely preferable to the alternatives exercised by some countries.

Before joining the Common Market, Great Britain had been wrestling for some time with the problem of remaining a small independent nation in a world that was composing itself into ever larger groupings that reflected their own interests. Dean Acheson, that most perceptive of post-war American statesmen, passed a remark to the effect that Britain had lost an empire but had not yet found a role to play.

Although this role may yet be found within Europe, such considerations are pointless if only because today's speculation will be tomorrow's history, and recording that is a duty for the next generation.

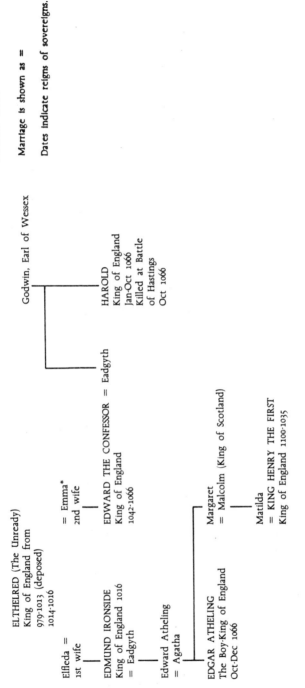

Godwin, Earl of Wessex

HAROLD
King of England
Jan-Oct 1066
Killed at Battle
of Hastings
Oct 1066

ELTHELRED (The Unready)
King of England from
979-1013 (deposed)
1014-1016

= Emma*
2nd wife

EDWARD THE CONFESSOR = Eadgyth
King of England
1042-1066

Elfleda =
1st wife

EDMUND IRONSIDE
King of England 1016
= Eadgyth

Edward Atheling
= Agatha

Margaret
= Malcolm (King of Scotland)

EDGAR ATHELING
The Boy-King of England
Oct-Dec 1066

Matilda
= KING HENRY THE FIRST
King of England 1100-1035

*Emma (Daughter of Richard, Duke of Normandy) married as her second husband King Canute
who reigned as King of England 1016-1035, his two sons succeeded as Kings of England, Harold
Harefoot 1037-1040, and Hardincanute 1040-1042.

**Gytha claimed royal descent from King Sweyn Forkbeard, King of England 1013-1014, having
briefly deposed King Elthelred.

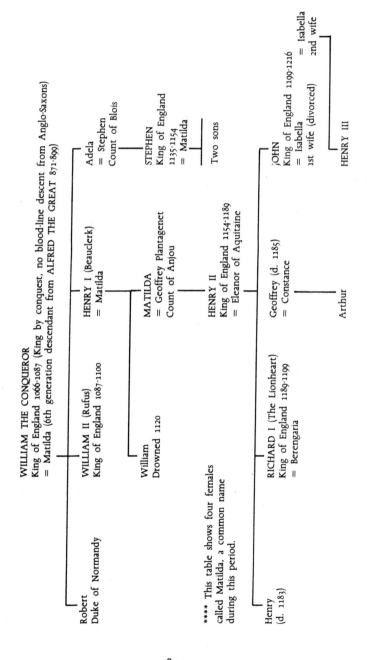

WILLIAM THE CONQUEROR
King of England 1066-1087 (King by conquest, no blood-line descent from Anglo-Saxons)
= Matilda (6th generation descendant from ALFRED THE GREAT 871-899)

Robert
Duke of Normandy

WILLIAM II (Rufus)
King of England 1087-1100

William
Drowned 1120

HENRY I (Beauclerk)
= Matilda

MATILDA
= Geoffrey Plantagenet
Count of Anjou

HENRY II
King of England 1154-1189
= Eleanor of Aquitaine

Adela
= Stephen
Count of Blois

STEPHEN
King of England
1135-1154
= Matilda

Two sons

**** This table shows four females
called Matilda, a common name
during this period.

Henry
(d. 1183)

RICHARD I (The Lionheart)
King of England 1189-1199
= Berengaria

Geoffrey (d. 1185)
= Constance

Arthur

JOHN
King of England 1199-1216
= Isabella
1st wife (divorced)
= Isabella
2nd wife

HENRY III

189

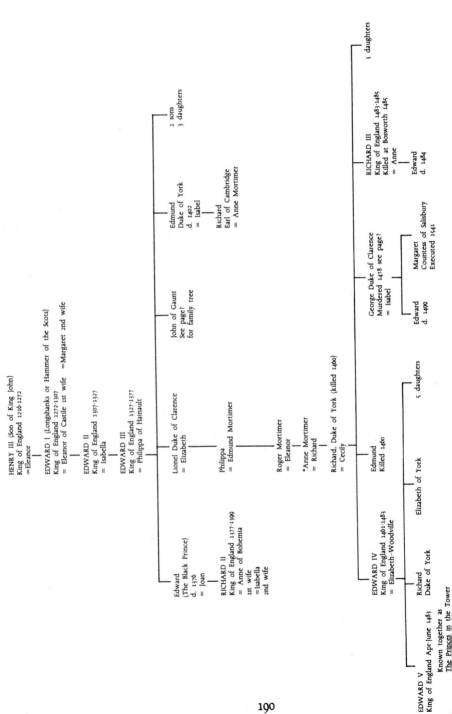

HENRY III (Son of King John)
King of England 1216-1272
=Eleanor

EDWARD I (Longshanks or Hammer of the Scots)
King of England 1272-1307
= Eleanor of Castile 1st wife   =Margaret 2nd wife

EDWARD II
King of England 1307-1327
= Isabella

EDWARD III
King of England 1327-1377
= Philippa of Hainault

Edward
(The Black Prince)
d. 1376
= Joan

Lionel Duke of Clarence
= Elizabeth

John of Gaunt
See page?
for family tree

Edmund
Duke of York
d. 1402

2 sons
3 daughters

RICHARD II
King of England 1377-1399
= Anne of Bohemia
1st wife
=Isabella
2nd wife

Philippa
= Edmund Mortimer

Richard
Earl of Cambridge
= Anne Mortimer

Roger Mortimer
= Eleanor

*Anne Mortimer
= Richard

Richard, Duke of York (killed 1460)
= Cecily

Edmund
Killed 1460

George Duke of Clarence
Murdered 1478 see page?
= Isabel

RICHARD III
King of England 1483-1485
Killed at Bosworth 1485
= Anne

EDWARD IV
King of England 1461-1483
= Elizabeth-Woodville

Elizabeth of York

5 daughters

Edward
d. 1499

Margaret
Countess of Salisbury
Executed 1541

Edward
d. 1484

Richard
Duke of York

3 daughters

EDWARD V
King of England Apr-June 1483

Known together as
The Princes in the Tower

190

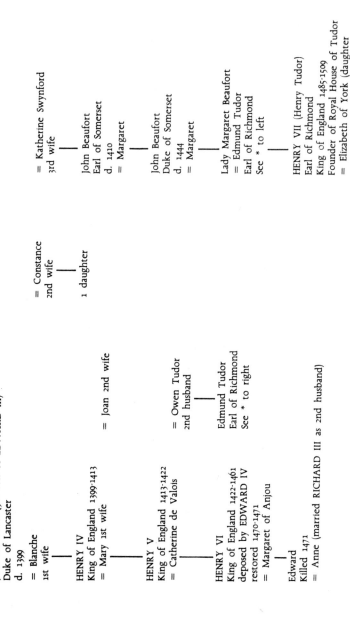

John of Gaunt (3rd son of EDWARD III)
Duke of Lancaster
d. 1399
= Blanche
1st wife
= Constance
2nd wife
= Katherine Swynford
3rd wife

1 daughter

John Beaufort
Earl of Somerset
d. 1410
= Margaret

HENRY IV
King of England 1399-1413
= Mary 1st wife
= Joan 2nd wife

HENRY V
King of England 1413-1422
= Catherine de Valois
= Owen Tudor
2nd husband

John Beaufort
Duke of Somerset
d. 1444
= Margaret

Edmund Tudor
Earl of Richmond
See * to right

Lady Margaret Beaufort
= Edmund Tudor
Earl of Richmond
See * to left

HENRY VI
King of England 1422-1461
deposed by EDWARD IV
restored 1470-1471
= Margaret of Anjou

HENRY VII (Henry Tudor)
Earl of Richmond
King of England 1485-1509
Founder of Royal House of Tudor
= Elizabeth of York (daughter

Edward
Killed 1471
= Anne (married RICHARD III as 2nd husband)

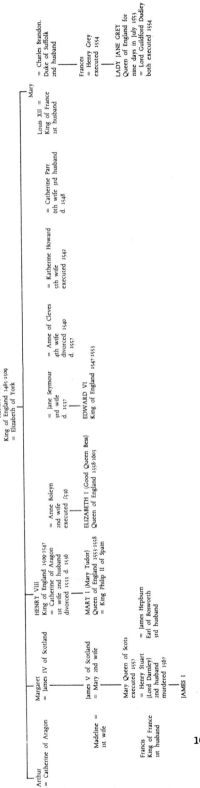

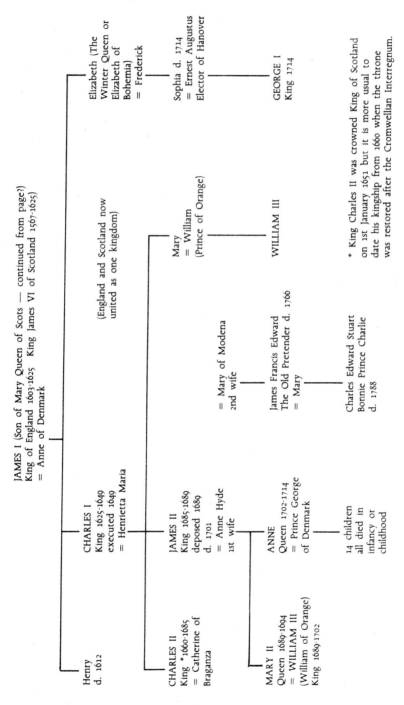

JAMES I (Son of Mary Queen of Scots — continued from page?)
King of England 1603-1625 King James VI of Scotland 1567-1625)
= Anne of Denmark

CHARLES I
King 1625-1649
executed 1649
= Henrietta Maria

Elizabeth (The
Winter Queen or
Elizabeth of
Bohemia)
= Frederick

(England and Scotland now
united as one kingdom)

Sophia d. 1714
= Ernest Augustus
Elector of Hanover

Henry
d. 1612

CHARLES II
King *1660-1685
= Catherine of
Braganza

JAMES II
King 1685-1689
deposed 1689
d. 1701
= Anne Hyde
1st wife

= Mary of Modena
2nd wife

Mary
= William
(Prince of Orange)

GEORGE I
King 1714

MARY II
Queen 1689-1694
= WILLIAM III
(William of Orange)
King 1689-1702

ANNE
Queen 1702-1714
= Prince George
of Denmark

James Francis Edward
The Old Pretender d. 1766
= Mary

WILLIAM III

14 children
all died in
infancy or
childhood

Charles Edward Stuart
Bonnie Prince Charlie
d. 1788

* King Charles II was crowned King of Scotland
on 1st January 1651 but it is more usual to
date his kingship from 1660 when the throne
was restored after the Cromwellian Interregnum.

193

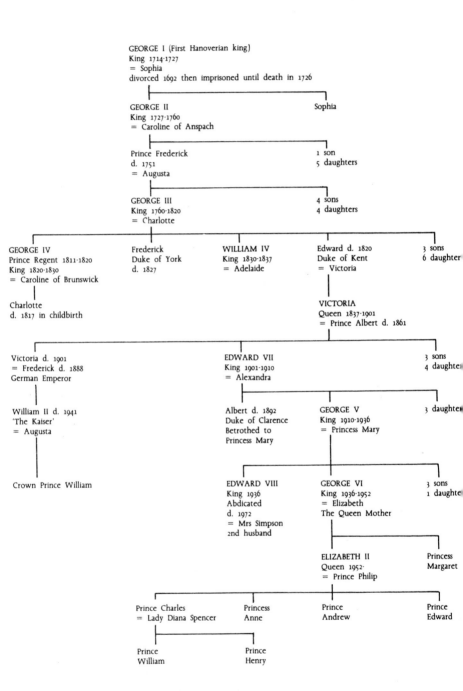

GEORGE I (First Hanoverian king)
King 1714-1727
= Sophia
divorced 1692 then imprisoned until death in 1726

GEORGE II   Sophia
King 1727-1760
= Caroline of Anspach

Prince Frederick   1 son
d. 1751   5 daughters
= Augusta

GEORGE III   4 sons
King 1760-1820   4 daughters
= Charlotte

GEORGE IV   Frederick   WILLIAM IV   Edward d. 1820   3 sons
Prince Regent 1811-1820 Duke of York   King 1830-1837   Duke of Kent   6 daughter
King 1820-1830   d. 1827   = Adelaide   = Victoria
= Caroline of Brunswick

Charlotte   VICTORIA
d. 1817 in childbirth   Queen 1837-1901
                                                           = Prince Albert d. 1861

Victoria d. 1901   EDWARD VII   3 sons
= Frederick d. 1888   King 1901-1910   4 daughter
German Emperor   = Alexandra

William II d. 1941   Albert d. 1892   GEORGE V   3 daughter
'The Kaiser'   Duke of Clarence   King 1910-1936
= Augusta   Betrothed to   = Princess Mary
                                        Princess Mary

                                        EDWARD VIII   GEORGE VI   3 sons
Crown Prince William   King 1936   King 1936-1952   1 daughter
                                        Abdicated   = Elizabeth
                                        d. 1972   The Queen Mother
                                        = Mrs Simpson
                                        2nd husband

                                                           ELIZABETH II   Princess
                                                           Queen 1952-   Margaret
                                                           = Prince Philip

          Prince Charles   Princess   Prince   Prince
          = Lady Diana Spencer   Anne   Andrew   Edward

          Prince   Prince
          William   Henry